# STRATEGIES for TRANSITIONS to RETIREMENT (2nd edition)

A comprehensive study on retirement concerns of today!

**Mary Gallinger**, B.Sc. Chem. Eng., M.A. Leadership & Training

Focus Group comments... "Everyone needs to read this rich, rewarding and thought-provoking book for much success and happiness in retirement life."

## WWW.RETIREMENTREADY.NET

OTHER SERVICES AVAILABLE...

WORKSHOPS: Full-day or customized interactive workshops available.

TELECLASSES: "Transitions to Retirement" available via telephone.

PUBLICATIONS:
Quarterly Newsletter,
101 Tips for Retirement and
You can feel it in their voices: inspirational stories to nurture the soul!

D0892769

**Canadian Cataloguing in Publication Data**

Gallinger, Mary, 1957-
  Strategies for transitions to retirement

Includes bibliographical references and index.
ISBN 1-55212-442-8

  1. Retirement--Planning. I. Title.
HQ1062.G34 2000          646.7'9          C00-910942-0

# TRAFFORD

**This book was published *on-demand* in cooperation with Trafford Publishing.**
On-demand publishing is a unique process and service of making a book available for retail sale to the public taking advantage of on-demand manufacturing and Internet marketing.
**On-demand publishing** includes promotions, retail sales, manufacturing, order fulfilment, accounting and collecting royalties on behalf of the author.

Suite 6E, 2333 Government St., Victoria, B.C. V8T 4P4, CANADA
Phone      250-383-6864          Toll-free    1-888-232-4444 (Canada & US)
Fax        250-383-6804          E-mail      sales@trafford.com
Web site    www.trafford.com    TRAFFORD PUBLISHING IS A DIVISION OF TRAFFORD HOLDINGS LTD.
Trafford Catalogue #00-0107      www.trafford.com/robots/00-0107.html

10        9        8        7

# TABLE OF CONTENTS

# PREFACE

Are you ready for retirement? How can individuals plan for the gradual shift from working to retirement? How can they make the psychological transition from working full time to not working?

There is a recognized need for information to support the aging population heading to retirement. Many retirees become ill within a year of leaving work because they fail to plan for a gradual shift from working to retirement. Individuals with outside interests are at less risk than executives who have been accustomed to spending 80 hours a week on the job, but even hobbies and interests have to be refined prior to retirement. For many people, one of the most profound periods of change is their time of retirement. People's needs and attitudes are different, however, no matter what their personal goals, current age and economic circumstances may be, the strategies they employ to plan for a satisfying retirement are crucial to their mental happiness, physical health and general survival. These strategies will either enhance the quality of their golden years or shorten them drastically.

This book contains literature reviews on change, the history of retirement, stages of aging and the achievement of balance in life. Focus groups and one-on-one interviews were conducted with participants considering retirement, participants retired less than five years and more than five years. This book includes recommendations for the organization, for the individual and for future research.  As qualitative research in particular relies on the words of participants and the observations of the researcher to express reality, the information gained from these interviews assisted the researcher in developing new and creative approaches to retirement transition based on the words of those considering retirement and in retirement transition.  These approaches are outlined as strategies for transitions to retirement.

## **DEDICATION**

This research project is dedicated to my father, the late Harry Paryniuk, whose personal life experiences, love for humankind and wisdom, fed my passion and provided me with encouragement to conduct this research study to make a difference!

This book is written for everyone facing retirement transition. May this book be a source of inspiration and comfort.

Much love and happiness to all!

Mary Gallinger

# ACKNOWLEDGEMENTS

There are many people to whom I owe a debt of gratitude in the completion of this research and book.

To my husband Hugh and daughter Christine for their understanding and support during my long hours of research and writing. I love you forever.

To my mother Dunja and brother Harry for their unconditional love and on-going support. I love you forever.

To all of the participants who volunteered their time to participate in the interview process and opened their hearts and shared their personal life stories with me. The opportunity to dialogue your learning face-to-face during the one-on-one interviews and focus group sessions was such a powerful and moving experience for me. It also provided an opportunity of inspiration and growth. Thank you for sharing your life with me.

Much love and happiness to you all!

Mary Gallinger

# CHAPTER ONE - BACKGROUND

## The Problem/Opportunity

During the post-war period from 1947 until the mid 1960's, Canadians produced roughly 400,000 babies each year, peaking at 500,000 in 1960. This baby boomer generation, which represents a disproportionate chunk of the population, has been the leading force behind social, cultural and economic changes in Canada during the last four decades. Statistics indicate that by 2011, one in five Canadians will be over 65 years of age as compared to one in ten in the early 1990's. Canada, like many other countries, is experiencing a significant aging of its population. This trend is expected to lead to an increase in demands on public sector funds for pensions, health care and seniors' programs. These demands are dependent on demographic change, economic growth and structural aspects of the public sector age-sensitive programs. The baby boomers are heading to retirement. Data suggests that Canadians are continuing to take a last-minute approach to retirement. (Statistics Canada, 1990)

Since World War II, larger percentages of our able-bodied population have withdrawn from the labor force or retired early. Baby boomers will soon reach retirement age. As a result, labor shortages, increasing dependency ratios, lower standards of living will be important in the first part of the twenty-first century. This raises a number of critical questions about the nature of retirement now and in the past.

The University of Victoria Center on Aging Team suggests that society is diligent about mandatory retirement and treats seniors as retired from life when they leave the workplace. Fears about dementia and about becoming institutionalized and decrepit are not justified. The Director of the Center, Neena Chappell, states that:

> Despite these fears, 8% of Canadian Seniors suffer from dementia, as there is a 1 in 3 chance of dementia over the age of 85 years; 7% of seniors 65 or over end up in an institution; Pacific Coast Internet service provider shows that one third of their customers are seniors, and seniors are more physically active than we recognize.
> (Victoria Times Colonist, Monday May 10, 1999, p. A-6)

The sheer volume of advertising and media coverage of retirement savings opportunities sends a clear message that the population is aging. Mass marketers are shifting their focus to cater to the aging population as baby boomers begin to enter retirement. An awareness of the trends in an aging population leads to the need for retirement planning and has helped turn the financial industry into the growth industry of the decade. This aging population will place a huge strain on the Canada Pension Plan (CPP) / Quebec Pension Plan, and with fewer people in the workforce, the Canadian tax base will be smaller. This will further stretch pension programs and the health care system. With this in mind, the focus on financial institutions is increasingly shifting to retirement savings. Because there is less money to go around, it has become more important for Canadians to save and invest wisely. Baby boomers must take charge of their futures or pay the consequences later in life. Unfortunately, most people do not begin planning for retirement until just before they retire. Research from Statistics Canada (1990) indicates that over 60% of Canadians will retire on CPP and old age security alone. The general practice in retirement planning involves estimating the cost of the lifestyle one will likely want to lead upon retirement. Beyond this, individuals must estimate their income needs, taking into account inflation, current assets, and time remaining until retirement. Inflation is an important issue as it could potentially erode half of one's spending power in a 15-year period of time.

The goal of this project is to conduct research into the questions: **Are you ready for retirement? How can individuals plan for the gradual shift from working to retirement? How can they make the psychological transition from working full time to not working?**

Many retirees become ill within a year of leaving work because they fail to plan for a gradual shift from working to retirement. Individuals with outside interests are at less risk than executives who have been used to spending 80 hours a week on the job, but even hobbies and interests may have to be refined upon retirement.

Based on my discussions with people, I believe this research has the potential of making a significant contribution to the body of knowledge on transition to retirement. If the issues are not resolved, we will certainly see and hear of more people suffering through retirement. The research will also benefit the target sponsor and participants. It will suggest approaches to leadership that can be of use in the management of change in this era of turmoil and downsizing. It will also provide me an opportunity to engage others in a problem- solving process and to display leadership. The result of this action research project is to provide information to inform people of successful strategies for transitions to retirement.

Many people resist retirement because they feel too ashamed to face and deal with the issues involved, and even if they have a desire to retire, they feel helpless and hopeless as they search for adequate resolutions to their problems. Some people try to escape or avoid the issue, but the problem does not go away. People devote enormous amounts of energy to preparing financially for retirement, but too little thought is given to making sure they are psychologically prepared. If one simply stops working at age 65, one's health and happiness could be at risk. People can begin thinking about retirement as early as age 40, especially when lifetime work is not guaranteed and they can find themselves forced into early retirement.

## Significance of the Problem/Opportunity

Nineteen hundred and ninety-nine is the United Nations International Year of Older Persons. The present research is timely. It is part of a movement to engage participants in self-awareness for retirement. For many people, one of the most profound periods of change is the time of retirement. Early planning can help make the transition easier. People's needs and attitudes are different. However, no matter what their personal goals, current age and economic circumstances may be, the strategies they employ to plan for a satisfying retirement are crucial to their mental happiness, physical health and general survival. These strategies will either enhance the quality of their golden years or shorten them drastically. What are these strategies? If we simply buy the financial industry's image of the ideal retirement of endless beaches and golf, we are likely to face disappointment and boredom.

It is also a mistake to view retirement negatively, as a time when physical and mental abilities decline. If people are healthy the day before they retire, they are likely to be healthy the day after. Many retirees become ill within a year of leaving work because they fail to plan for a gradual shift from working to retirement. The risk is exacerbated if they combine retirement with other major life changes such as moving, marrying, divorcing, or taking on a large mortgage. Individuals with outside interests are at less risk than executives who have been used to spending 80 hours a week on the job, but even hobbies and interests may have to be refined upon retirement. People are usually most fulfilled when they have well-rounded lives that include work or work related activities. They need to include other activities in their lives as well such as volunteering, consulting, leisure activities such as sports, crafts, spiritual activities, community involvement, family, friendships, education and self-improvement. When individuals include these activities in their lives, they are enriched.

Retirement potentially provides people with many opportunities; it offers them ways to increase their passion for life! By means of engaging people in research, this study will provide the sharing of knowledge that could potentially enhance the quality of peoples' lives and enabling them to see constructive ways of becoming ready for retirement. The research will lead to the development of a list of strategies people can use to manage the psychological transition from working full time to not working.


## Potential Causes of the Problem/Opportunity

There is a stigmatism associated with retirement. Many common fears about aging are not justified. Awareness is the first step in recognizing these facts.  Chappell suggests:

> In the paradox of aging is that we age physically, on the outside, which suggests deterioration inside but inwardly we continue to evolve and grow. (Victoria Times Colonist, Monday May 10, 1999, p. A-6)


People often lack preparation and planning for the transition from working full time to not working. People may be offered early retirement packages even when they are not considering retirement. Companies may lay people off to make room for younger employees who have more years of work to offer.


Many people resist retirement because they feel too ashamed to face and deal with the issues involved.  And even if they have a desire to retire, they feel helpless and hopeless as they search for adequate resolutions to their problems.  Some people try to escape or avoid the issue. But the problem does not go away. Quite often it grows larger. This, in turn, causes more problems. In The Learning Paradox, Harris (1996) suggests that the adult addiction to feeling competent is futile because we need to adapt continuously to a world that is constantly shifting direction. He also says that "job loss is the primary fear among working Canadians and not even the best companies can offer job security for people in this changing environment." (p. 17)

There are many questions to consider. How can we handle these fears and changes as we get older and face retirement? Can we begin to think about the way we think, and become self-reflective, self-correcting and more creative? How can we create security in this changing environment? Does it stem from learning, changing and accepting uncertainty, the very things we as adults fear most?

Many people leave the process of planning for retirement until they are nearing retirement. This may cause undue stress and anxiety. They say they want to do certain things when they retire, but because they have not done the necessary planning they can't do these things. When it comes to retirement, almost any decision carries short-term and long-term consequences, and the two are often diametrically opposed. A solution is implemented which alleviates the problem. But the unintended consequences of the solution actually worsen the performance or condition, which one is attempting to correct. Senge et al (1994) calls this a "fix that fails." (p. 127)

Sometimes people are aware of the negative consequences of applying a quick fix. They do it anyway because the pain of not doing something right away is more urgent and feels more powerful than the delayed negative effects. The relief is temporary and the symptoms return, often worse than

before. This happens because the unintended consequences snowball slowly over a long period of time, often unnoticed at first but continuing to accumulate as the wrong solution is applied repeatedly. In "fixes that fail," people feel powerlessness when confronted with the consequences of their actions. People often see the dangers of what they are doing, but they feel they have no choice.

Graebner (1980) suggests that in many ways retirement is a fascinating case study of the birth and evolution of an economic institution. It is a history that, in it's telling, throws light on the complex nature and role of retirement as an institution. Wolozin (1990) says that in a fundamental sense, retirement is the product of preexisting concepts or theories about work, efficiency and age, manifested in part "as a political device imposed by one group on another."

(p. 1045) In its inception, retirement was a concept largely born of conflict rather than benevolence of age group conflict, technological conflict, political conflict and ideological conflict. Wolozin believes retirement is a mythology or mystique. It is also an excuse for ageism and compassionate mannerisms. Retirement exacts a mounting toll in the psychological and social lives of a large number of older persons. As this happens, it will threaten the standards of living of the total population well into the twenty-first century.

# CHAPTER TWO – RELATED LITERATURE

## Review of Supporting Literature

A literary review of retirement reveals some common problems or issues. The evolution or history of retirement, stages of aging, adaptations to change and the achievement of a balanced life are important aspects of retirement literature, and are also integral to this research study.

## History of Retirement

This literature review on the history of retirement will cover areas of research connected with evolution, demographics, societal contexts and future implications.

## Evolution

Wolozin (1981) submits that the average Canadian born 100 years ago did not experience retirement, as we know it today. Retirement is an invention, which has become popular only in this century. Young people who entered the labor force in 1900 would not expect to retire at the age of 65. Most did not do so. Wolozin suggests that retirement is another aspect of the structure of life course. These structural issues have both social and psychological impacts. The impacts of a given life course event on an individual will vary depending on how much he or she anticipates and interprets the events, and on how typical one's particular life course is in comparison to the norm. Most people live beyond the time they expect to live. In terms of retirement, many people live their working lives without giving much thought to or preparation for the fact that they can anticipate a very large number of years in retirement.

Graebner (1980) prompts that retirement is a fascinating case study of the birth and evolution of an economic institution. "It is a history that, in it's telling, throws light

on the complex nature and role of retirement as an institution." (p.1) Wolozin (1989) suggests that to fully understand and chart its evolution requires acknowledgment of the relevance and interaction of individual agency and social structure. Doing so supplies us with a critical methodological tool of contextual analysis that takes into account the dynamic and complete interaction of an organism within its context. In a fundamental sense, Wolozin (1990) describes:

> Retirement as the product of preexisting concepts or theories about work, efficiency and age, manifested in part as a political device imposed by one group on another. In its inception, retirement was a concept largely born of conflict, rather than of benevolence, of age group conflict, technological conflict, political conflict, and ideological conflict. (p. 1046)

Wolozin (1990) suggests that efficiency in the emerging technological society of the late nineteenth and early twentieth century was the key issue rationalizing retiring older workers. Among labor unions, it was in part a recruitment device--a benefit enticement for recruiting new members. It was also embraced as a method for making room for the advancement of younger members. Retirement was a political strategy invoked by government to cope with massive unemployment.

On another level, Wolozin (1990) insinuates that retirement was an institution nurtured by assumptions and interpretations of the aging process now shown to be highly questionable by current research on life-span development. "Originally based in large part on prejudice, ageism is a fundamental sense this society's non-rational and confused response to old age." (p. 1046)

In anthropological research, Keith and Van Nosh (1980) describe retirement as a cultural rite of passage, which does not yield to a simple explanation or interpretation in our society. Retirement in our society, particularly in its early development, has been largely viewed and rationalized as an economic phenomenon rather than a cultural rite of passage. However, Wolozin (1990) states, that:

> Retirement has also become in part a
> misguided version of an economic
> phenomenon through the development by
> the mid-1950 of what I dubbed in an earlier
> paper the retirement-pension mystique.
> (p.1047)

Graebner (1980) describes this as the "retirement
mythology" (p. 251) Keith and Van Nosh (1980)
describes this as a "roleless role" (p. 358)

In a seminal study of the history of retirement,
Graebner (1980) concluded that:

> Retirement has had no single function in
> American history. It served during the
> various stages of its development, as a tool
> of efficiency, modernization,
> depersonalization, age discrimination,
> personal security, social welfare, and
> unemployment relief. (p. 263)

The study of the history of retirement shows that
it was virtually non-existent before 1890 and only
a marginal institution at that time. By 1920 it
had become an important one. Not only did it
become significant in the three decades between
these years and grow rapidly after that, it became
a threat to both older workers and middle-age
workers. Graebner (1980) reported that by the
1920s, machinists who had not yet reached middle
age "...Felt compelled to deceive their employers
by dyeing their hair..." (p. 24)

In the 1920's the average age of death was much younger than it is now in the year 2000. People now live longer and this in itself has created more years of retirement life. In the 1920's mandatory retirement was a manifestation of ageism, flourishing as a means of getting rid of older workers. Graebner (1980) reported that by 1925 retirement was viewed and interpreted as "a realistic" solution to unemployment as well as a path to allegedly increase workforce productivity. Underlying all of this was an explicit assumption that old age was a period of declining abilities and skills.

Graebner (1980) suggests that in the early part of the twentieth century, retirement systems spread: the railroad workers, federal employees, union members, and teachers all came under retirement systems. During 1935 in North America, the landmark Social Security Act legitimized 65 as the retirement age and brought the bulk of American workers into the retirement fold. Although this act was hailed as a welfare measure on a national scale, its immediate objectives were narrowly economic. It was conceived as a way to achieve unemployment relief, increase productivity, and stimulate consumption. It served as a counter cyclical tool and responded to what was conceived to be a longer-term structural problem. Some people believed that technology undermined the job market for older workers and created long-term unemployment, and that in the future, older workers would need to be removed from the labor market rather than brought back into it. In addition, there was no thought given to what people would do once they retired. There was no concern over what retirement would mean for the retired person. The Social Security Act was focused on the economic role of retirement, conceived as a social tool for securing such objectives as unemployment relief and efficiency. The view of retirement had not yet reached the stage in which it was conceptualized as a period of leisure, granted as a reward for a lifetime of work. The total experience of the retired person was of little concern to policy makers

Herz and Rones (1989) prompts that the Social Security legislation set the stage for what became by the second half of the century a major development--the steady trend toward early retirement since the post-World War II period. A number of studies concluded that the earnings test built into the Social Security system was a substantial disincentive to work, reinforced by the establishment of widespread early incentive plans in the private sector. Even the 1983 Social Security amendments, designed to remove work disincentives, seemed to have little success in reversing this trend. The choice for older workers is most often between continuing full time in a long-held job or withdrawing from the labor force. Their age bars them from changing jobs. Even though more recent psychological research suggests that what older workers may need is change rather than retirement. Age discrimination bars them from new full-time jobs. Low wages and lack of fringe benefits like health insurance lead the majority of older workers to reject part-time employment. In other words, age discrimination bars older workers from changing jobs and forces them into retirement.

## Demographics

Marshall (1993) indicates Canada has an aging population. At the beginning of this century less than six percent of the Canadian population was aged 65 and older. Today more than ten percent fall into that category, and by 2031 this proportion will rise to almost 25 percent. The proportion that will be old by the decades 2021 and 2031 is now projected to be considerably higher than had been believed 15 or 20 years ago because demographers no longer anticipate large increases in fertility, and because recent decreases in later-life mortality are significant.

Wolfson et al (1990) insinuate that Canada - like many other countries - is experiencing a significant aging of its population. This trend is expected to increase the burden on the public sector of major cash transfer and "in-kind" benefit programs. The estimated size of the burden depends on projections of demographic change, economic growth and structural aspects of the major age-sensitive public-sector programs. The burdens are analyzed for 2016 and 2036 when the period of demographic aging is expected to have the most impact on old-age dependency ratios and public-sector program costs. Contrary to many expressed concerns, demographic aging is not the most important factor in determining future public-sector costs and revenues. Aspects of the design and management of public-sector programs represent the greatest area of uncertainty. These areas are more amenable to public policy initiatives and gradual adjustments within the half-century time frame of the projections.

Foot (1993) forecasts that the aging process is expected to continue. Statistics Canada projections suggest that the source population will age on average approximately 3.2 years (or eight percent) over the final decade of the twentieth century. This is a significant increase. Calculations suggest the labor force median age will increase from 36.2 years to 38.8 years over the same period. This increase of 2.6 years is up from 2.5 years over the previous decade and suggests an increase in the pace of aging of the Canadian labor force over the 1990s. This aging has been a new development over the 1980s and the accelerated pace of labor force aging is likely to have important implications in the 1990s and beyond.

Marshall (1993) suggests that women live much longer than men. While life expectancy at birth is just 70.2 years for men, it is 77.5 years for women. These life expectancy differences persist at later ages. To illustrate, a man born in 1980 - 82 has a 75 percent chance of living to age 65. A woman born in that period has an 86 percent chance. At age 65, a man can expect to live an additional 14.6 years, whereas a woman can expect to live an additional 18.9 years. Women have an increased advantage in life expectancy over men. The world of the aged is becoming a world dominated by women. This has profound implications for women, who become a majority group, and for men, who become the new minority. This shift in the sex ratio has a profound impact on younger cohorts of the population in terms of economic support and the care-giving that may be needed, and on such public policy areas as housing, transportation, community support, health promotion and health care.

Marshall (1993) hints to another important aspect of the age structure of Canada's population as the changing median age. This is the age at which you would say half of all Canadians are younger than this age. The current median age of the Canadian population is 30. In 1971 it was just 26.2 years. By the end of this century it is projected that it will rise to 37.2 years. By 2031 when all the baby boomers are old, the median age may be as high as 41.6 years. As a larger proportion of our population reaches age 65 and beyond, the overall composition of Canadian society will become more mature.

Bean et al (1983) suggest another interesting and important trend that is considered as a population in it, the group over age 65 is aging. Growth in the numbers among the very advanced ages over 80 occurs at a greater rate than among the younger old people ages 61 to 70 years. This will change after 2010, when the first of the baby boomers start to enter the 65 categories. By 2031, about one in 20 Canadians will be aged 85 or older.

## Societal Contexts

Lazear (1979) submits those most large organizations and many small ones used mandatory retirement ages, until it was made illegal (in most cases) by the United States Age Discrimination in Employment Act of 1974 and amendments to it in 1979. This presented a puzzle to economists. Similar comments can be made in Canada. Lazear (1979) wonders:

> Why should a firm that was willing to pay a worker $1000 per week be unwilling to employ that worker at any price in the next week, merely because the worker had turned 65? Surely productivity could not fall in such a discontinuous fashion. (p. 89)

There were a number of attempts to explain this phenomenon in non-economic terms, but none was truly coherent. For example, some claimed that mandatory retirement was a way to ease out old workers without affecting company morale. But the knowledge that retirement is imminent may affect morale more adversely than a pay reduction with the option of staying on beyond the normal retirement age.

The explanation in Lazear (1979) takes a very different approach. There, it is argued that earnings should grow more rapidly than productivity as the worker acquires experience. In effect, young workers are paid less than they are worth and old workers are paid more. By doing this in a way that keeps the present value of lifetime productivity, incentives are provided to workers that would be absent if they were to be paid a wage that followed life-cycle productivity more closely. The reason is that if workers reduce their effort, the risk of termination increases, and the workers would then forfeit the expected higher pay in the future.

Lazear (1979) suggests, suppose a worker who works at the efficient level of effort has an even productivity profile over his career. Suppose further that he has alternative use of time such as the value of leisure, which increases over the worker's lifetime. If wages were paid strictly according to productivity, then efficient retirement would occur when the value of leisure time exceeded the productivity of the worker. The present value of the wage payment must equal the present value of productivity over the life of the worker, or either the firm or the worker would seek a different partner for its labor contract. If the worker were offered a constant wage over his life, instead of a rising wage, he would be more likely to reduce productivity as his retirement age approaches. If a worker reduces productivity, the worst thing that could happen is that he is fired. But the worker still picks up the value of his leisure, which is equal to productivity and to the wage. So reducing productivity one year before costs nothing since retirement will happen next year regardless, and yields the benefit of increased utility from reduced effort. The cost of reducing productivity is much higher if the worker is offered a steadily rising wage. The lower initial wage indicates that over the entire lifetime, the firm breaks even. The worker's reputation maintains them from being terminated. As the worker's productivity increases, so does their rate of pay. A profile with wage increases over a lifetime results in higher lifetime productivity and higher lifetime wages. Workers prefer higher wage profiles.

Efficient wage arrangements require an increase in wages to provide motivation against shrinking and loss of productivity. It requires mandatory retirement since workers who face a rising wage profile will not chose to leave at the efficient age, when the value of leisure exceeds their productivity. An efficient contract is designed such that the present value of wages paid equals the present value of output. Work beyond retirement age implies that the firm takes losses. Mandatory retirement is only mandatory in the sense that workers prefer to keep receiving wages that are higher than their actual level of productivity. But these same workers would prefer the rising wage profile with mandatory retirement as compared to a flat wage profile. The rising wage profile results in higher lifetime earnings as workers make decisions on effort per hour and hours per lifetime. A wage profile that induces an efficient level of effort per year or per hour will also guarantee an efficient choice of hours per lifetime. Institutions that look like hour constraints, either in the form of mandatory retirement or daily restrictions on hours worked, can bring about efficiency on this dimension. This explanation for mandatory retirement is based on optimization of behavior and is supported by the data. Lazear (1979) found that mandatory retirement is associated positively with job tenure and wage growth. Long-term jobs tend to use mandatory retirement and those with age-earning profiles that rise tend to have mandatory retirement. Mandatory retirement occurred primarily at age 65. This is when social security assistance is provided. These functions are consistent with the argument that mandatory retirement is reserved for those for whom wages exceed marginal products.

More evidence on how upward-sloping wage profiles are used for incentives is provided by Hutchens (1986, 1987). First, Hutchens finds that steep profiles are used for workers who are hired when young rather than old. He argues that the up-front implicit payment from worker to firm is like a fixed cost that workers are unlikely to pay unless the expected tenure is long. Workers hired early are more likely to have steeply rising wage profiles, mandatory retirement and pensions. Second, Hutchens (1987) matches his information from the Dictionary of Occupational Titles with the National Longitudinal Survey. He finds that jobs where it is cheap to monitor effort frequently are not the jobs that have mandatory retirement, pensions or steep profiles. When monitoring is costly, jobs are more likely to use the upward-sloping profile as a substitute for incentive schemes.

## Future Implications

Foot (1993) indicates that the Canadian labor force went through dramatic changes over the 1970s and 1980s. The nature of the changes and the associated labor market challenges are now gradually emerging. A slowing source population growth and increase in average age are the dominant and most critical features of Canada's future labor force. These have far reaching implications with respect to the successful utilization of this essential national resource.

Foot (1993) submits that in 1981 there were over three million youth in the Canadian labor market "25.8 percent of the labor force." Over the 1960s, and especially the 1970s, the challenges for the labor market primarily centered on job creation and successful absorption of the massive baby-boomer generation into the Canadian labor force without undo pressures on unemployment rates. This was largely accomplished by the mid - 1980s.

Foot (1993) indicates in 1991 the number of youth (15 to 24 years) fell by 575,000 persons and their share of the labor force dropped to 18.2 percent. This trend continued into the 1990s. By the mid-1990s participation rates did not change. The baby-boom echo generation entered the Canadian labor force. Supplemented by immigration, youth numbers gradually increased over the second half of the 1990s. However, at unchanged participation rates, by 2001 the number will barely reach the 1990 level and they will represent 17 percent of the Canadian labor force. This means that organizations will be faced with relatively fewer younger people from which to recruit for their entry-level positions. There are a number of labor market implications resulting from the lack of new blood in organizations. Traditionally, new or young labor market participants fill entry-level positions in an organization. These persons are presumed to be the most flexible with respect to mobility and occupation. They possess up-to-date labor market skills and do not have a work history tying them to any particular organization or occupation. They are not already part of an organization's bureaucracy and culture and represent resources that can be deployed in a most efficient manner without disruptive costs to both employer and employee. Without this flexibility, what are the alternative options available to organizations? Using computer simulation experiments in the 1990's it was confirmed that promotion prospects are related positively to the rate of population growth and to the age of retirement. It is related negatively to population aging and the age of labor force entrance. The baby boomers suffer some disadvantage as a result of their sheer numbers. The first baby boomers, born in 1947, reached age 45 in 1992. The aging population weakens promotion prospects considerably. There may be increased discontentment in the Canadian labor force in the years ahead. This discontentment may make the effective utilization of existing resources more difficult and could facilitate such re deployment as employees move in an attempt to seek new challenges. Organizations will have to adapt and respond to this new labor market environment.

## Stages of aging

This literature review describes the stages of aging encompassing life span development, cognitive functions and health.

## Aging

Saxon and Etten (1978) suggest that as more of our population ages, gerontologists and providers of services to older persons are finding it necessary to redefine the concept of old age. Neugarten (1975) suggests that it is more appropriate to think of those who are 55 to 74 as the young-old and those who are 75 and older as the old-old. Most service providers agree that the needs are different in the young-old and old-old groups. Services and programs need to be structured, planned, orientated and delivered in different ways to service appropriate needs of both groups. Randall (1977) emphasizes the broad chronological age range of the elderly today by suggesting the following categories: very-young-old (50 to 60), young-old (61 to 70), middle-aged-old (71 to 80), very old old (81 to 99) and centenarians for the increasing number of those who are 100 and over. Both Neugarten (1975) and Randall (1977) agree that chronological age is not an accurate predictor of physical condition and behavior. They suggest attention to the great diversity in the group we call old and acknowledge the differences that must be made for this large, heterogeneous segment of the population if we are to provide effectively for human needs throughout these stages.

Saxon and Etten (1978) propose that people become unique, as they grow older, not more alike. Aging is a distinct part of the life cycle not yet experienced personally by most of those who work with the elderly. To understand the behavior of aged persons is difficult for many in the helping professions. Randall (1977) sums up the need as follows:

> The greatest priority for older people is the ability and opportunity to create a quality of living that is consonant with an individual's wishes. This takes more than just money - and often does not take money at all. It takes understanding of that which gives satisfaction in being alive. (p. 10)

Aging should be viewed in a developmental perspective, as a natural part of the life cycle, with many experiences of earlier years as well as present life situations all contributing to behavior in the later years. Bromley (1974) suggests, "We spend about one quarter of our lives growing up and three quarters growing old." (p. 9)

Saxon and Etten (1978) suggest:

> ...It seems strange then, that psychologists and others interested in human development have devoted the majority of their efforts to the study of childhood and adolescence. (p. 9)

Marshall (1993) prompts as aging progresses people become more aware that their own time on earth is limited. Marshall (1993) suggests that the vast majority of older people come to terms with their mortality, but that such concerns do not become salient for most people until some time in their seventies. At that time they experience more of their peers dying, and they become concerned that their own death be "appropriate." Most people do not want to live forever. They want to die feeling that they had a meaningful and dignified life. That is why the ability to remain independent, both physically and economically, and the ability to maintain family and affectionate bonds, is so critically important to the aged.

## Life Span Development

Erikson (1963) proposes one classification of developmental tasks ranging from the development of a sense of basic trust versus a sense of mistrust in infancy to the development of a sense of ego integrity versus a sense of despair in old age. Saxon and Etten (1978) suggest the developmental perspective noted below by Brammer and Shostrom (1977) with added information from Neugarten (1968) concerning middle age periods.

0-2 Infancy: A stage of dependency as the infant learns to relate to their caregivers. These are the earliest experiences with human relationships.

2-3 Early Childhood: A stage of independence when the child acquires an increase sense of autonomy, independence and mastery. Walking and talking assist them in the exploration of the environment and in building more complex relationships with others. Toilet training becomes an extremely important skill to master in our culture because it is possibly the first time the child has to acquiesce to the demands of authority figures. The management of aggression is another culturally expected behavior at this time.

4-6 Middle Childhood:  Children begin to learn role taking, as the relevant task is to learn proper social roles of males and females.  Conscience development becomes a significant aspect of development at this age level.

6-10 Late Childhood:  Children enter a stage of conformity, as the child must learn to cope with new authority figures and heterogeneous peers as a result of school experiences.  A preference for friends and associations of the same sex is characteristic of this stage.

10-13 Preadolescence:  A transition stage, which dominates by adjustment to rapid physical growth, sexual maturation and increased efforts to become independent of family control.  The sense of individuality is usually strong but peer pressure and peer conformity begins to increase at this time.

13-20 Adolescence:  A significant synthesis stage extremely significant in our culture as the transition from child to adult occurs. Unfortunately our culture has no clearly defined or universally acceptable guidelines for determining when this transition is completed. Adults, especially parents may not behave consistently toward the adolescent who in one situation is considered to be an adult but in another similar situation may be treated as a child. Parents, friends, society nor the adolescent knows when the transition to adult status is complete. This uncertainty increases the possibility of conflict. During this stage many important life decisions are made such as career choices, education, marriage, parenthood, establishment of an independent life style and personal identity. Establishment of a firm sense of personal identity and independence becomes paramount at this time.

20-35 Early Adult: An experimentation stage where young people test their decisions against reality. For many it is the first opportunity for decisions made in the earlier stage to be tried out in real life situations. Young people begin to establish themselves as an independent young adult testing themselves against the realities of work, home, school, religious and recreational activities.

35-50 Middle Age: A consolidation stage. For many middle-aged it is a time for intensive reevaluation of life and themselves. Middle age involves a time of change perspective with the realization that half of one's life is over.

<u>45-60 Middle Age:</u>  An involution stage, which overlaps in age range with the consolidation stage.  The developmental emphasis here is on coping with the psychological implications of upcoming old age.  Menopause in women and climacteric changes in men, gray hair, wrinkles; lessened energy and stamina become the physical signs of aging.  Some middle-aged people may experience depression as a number of psychologically significant events start to cumulate as children leave home, career and financial abilities peak, awareness of physical signs of aging occurs, parents and friends begin to die and time perspective changes as half of life has been lived.  For those who fear old age and death, depression and psychological problems are likely to occur.  For those who perceive their lives as rewarding and fulfilling, middle age becomes a highly satisfying time.  Many cope by finding new interests, intensifying current interests and setting new priorities for use of time.  Others make drastic changes in their life style.  Divorce after 20 to 30 years of marriage is on the increase.  Some have a last fling of infidelity to prove their sexual libido and attractiveness.  Others experience an emotional breakdown.  One group of educated and articulate middle-aged studied by Neugarten (1968) stressed that:

> ... Middle age is a time of competence and mastery, the prime of life - a comfortable period of life indeed. (p.12)

60 and older: An evaluation stage. The majority of tasks of this older age stage become a review of one's life. This is a purposeful constructive effort to review one's life, put it into perspective and cope with cumulating losses that occur with the progression of aging. A sense of personal integrity, the comfort of a life well lived, and preparation for an easy death are important considerations during this time.

Saxon and Etten (1978) suggest that human behavior involves complex interrelationships between physical, psychological and social factors. The nature and significance of bio-psycho-social interrelationships change as aging occurs. Each person remains a unique and complex being throughout life and can only be properly understood from a holistic perspective.

## Dependency and independence

Marshall (1993) insinuates the majority of older people want to be independent for as long as possible. Women who are now old have spent much of their lives submerging their own identities, not to mention their energies, in the care and feeding of their husbands and families. In later life women's responsibilities often increase. Marshall (1993) suggests:

> The majority of men die, so to speak, in the arms of their spouse, while the majority of women are already widowed by the time they need assistance. This is one of the

factors, which, in addition to gender roles
definitions, leads to women providing the
majority of care to the elderly. (p. 8)

Marshall (1993) hints that living alone is in itself
a new challenge for countless older people, but it
is especially a challenge for older women. Studies
show that the aged are not lonelier than other age
groups. Significant minorities of people of all ages
are lonely. Marshall (1993) suggests that:

> ...Living alone is the preferred living
> arrangement of the majority of older
> widows and widowers, who rarely wish to
> live with an adult child. The challenge here
> as indicated by three papers by Haldemann
> and Wister, Alun Joseph and Anne Martin -
> Matthews, and Ellen Gee and Susan
> McDaniel note, is to provide environments
> as well as formal and informal support
> systems to assist these people to maintain
> their independence. (p. 8)

## Cognitive Functions

Marshall (1993) suggests that people will tell you:

> ...I'd rather die than lose my faculties. This
> speaks to an important concern of the aged.
> We ought not to forget the problems of
> cognitive decline in later life, but we also
> ought to reduce unwarranted fears in this
> area by noting that only about 14 percent of

any birth cohort will suffer serious cognitive decline or dementia (including Alzheimer's Disease) at a clinical level, before they die. In other words, the vast majority of older people die with their faculties intact. (p. 9)

Lerner (1984) advises that in the field of psychological gerontology:

...Aging is not a fixed general process of decline, but rather that the older organism retains considerable potential for variability and plasticity. (p. ix)

This finding is the product of a new perspective on human development that has emerged from what has been hailed as a major conceptual change in both developmental psychology and life-course sociology. Brim and Kagan (1980) suggests this conception of human development differs from most Western contemporary thought on the subject. The view that emerges is that humans have a capacity for change across the entire life span. It questions the traditional idea that the experiences of the early years, which have a demonstrated contemporaneous effect, necessarily constrain the characteristics of adolescence and adulthood. Brim and Kagan (1980) further suggest:

... There are important growth changes across the life span from birth to death, many individuals retain a great capacity for change and the consequences of the events of early childhood are continually transformed by later experiences, making the course of human development more open than many have believed. (p. 1)

Learner (1984) prompts that scholars working in this field do not maintain that plasticity is limitless; however, they do maintain that it is ever-present in life. Of particular interest to Baltes (1987), his research revealed the possibility of new forms of intelligence in adulthood and old age. Scholars have found that one type of intelligence, namely crystallized intelligence actually increases with age. Baltes (1987) suggests as pragmatics, this includes:

...The ability to synthesize, social intelligence, cultural knowledge and as the pragmatics of intelligence, concerns the context and knowledge-related application of the mechanics of intelligence. (p. 614)

Baltes (1987) suggests it has also been found that:

...Expertise in select facets of the pragmatics of intelligence can be maintained, transformed, or even newly acquired in the second half of life. (p. 615)

Dixon (1986) suggests the conditions necessary for this to take place are ones in which individuals

"...continue to practice and evolve their procedural and factual knowledge" (p. 139) As such, this has serious implications for the retired person who, in essence has ceased to practice in critical areas. In the case of the older worker, work is his practice; for the retiree, it was his practice.

Baltes (1987) recommends another area of singular relevance is the emerging study of wisdom defined as "expertise in the fundamental pragmatics of life" (p. 615) In this area of intelligence, older persons are reported to do very well. They exhibit knowledge systems "more elaborated than that of younger adults" (p. 615) In another area of selective efficacy, evidence reveals that older workers, even when their reaction times are slower, hold their own in typing by using a different combination of component skills.

Baltes (1987) indicates this perspective on human development has profound implications for retirement and economic policy in general. Lerner (1984) speculates that federal funding programs "...impact relatively quickly on health, cognitive and familial function variables associated with an individual" (p. 167)

Wolozin (1990) proposes two observations. First, the research on life-span development suggests that retirement is an invitation to stop developing and second, for society, retirement is both a deterioration and loss of a potentially valuable resource. Wolozin (1990) suggests that deterioration takes place not only as a result of lack of use of mental resources from lack of practice but that deterioration may be exacerbated by the frustration of the retired person at being unable to provide for the basic emotional needs that psychologists have found fundamental to healthy existence. These needs include attachment, object seeking and relations, communion, self-integrity, and the feeling of self. Wolozin (1990) suggests these in two earlier papers: "Psychoanalytic Perspectives on Economic Institutions," 1987, and "Culture, Psychology, and Institutions: A Contextual Approach to Economic Behavior," 1989.)

He suggests:

> ...Good shares of these needs are often fulfilled in the workplace. It also follows that, given the conditions for growth of intelligence, frustration of these basic needs, because of the retirement experience, has a negative effect on the plasticity of the retired person. Growing support for this conclusion comes from the research in the field of developmental psychology which points to a new conception of influences that extend throughout the life-span" (p. 1056)

McPherson (1990) suggests that chronological aging represents an approximate measure of the normative development or changes within an individual or age cohort. There are great variations in physical, emotional, social and psychological development between individuals. Chronological aging of people interacts with a societal history and a number of socio-demographic factors such as class, gender, ethnicity, education and place of residence. Functional aging is a more accurate measure of aging, since individual differences by age are considered. Functional aging reflects the relationship between biological maturation or deterioration and how well an individual can adapt and perform specific physical, social or cognitive tasks. Psychological aging involves the reaction to biological, cognitive, sensory, motor, emotional and behavior changes as well as the reaction to external environmental factors that influence behavior and lifestyle. Social aging involves patterns of interaction between the aging individual and the social structure. Many social positions are related to chronological age and individuals are expected to conform to the age-based norms associated with these positions. Social aging is also influenced by the size and composition of the social structure as it changes over time, by change within a society, and by cultural and sub-cultural variations in attitudes toward aging and the aged. A number of unsubstantiated beliefs about aging and the aged are accepted as fact. These myths may influence the societal context on aging.

McPherson (1990) suggests the meaning of aging; the status of the aged and the process of aging vary across cultures and subcultures and during historical periods. In hunting-and-gathering societies where there was a surplus of food, the older members generally held influential positions in the social, political and religious spheres of tribal life. They were considered to be a source of knowledge of rituals and survival skills. In rural, agrarian and peasant societies where the elderly own or control the land, power and status are retained until land is transferred to a son. It is frequently assumed that the elderly lose power and status when a society becomes industrialized and modernized. Even today there is conflicting evidence. In some societies the status of the elderly declined following modernization and in some, their status declined before modernization. Usually after an industrial revolution the status remained at the pre-modernized level and in some the status declined at the onset of modernization. Alternatively, in some, their status declined initially following modernization and eventually increased after social and technological changes took place. Where support of aging parents is a cultural or subculture norm, it may not be the preferred pattern. As a result, the quality of the relationship may be low and the physical, emotional or psychological needs of the aging parents may not be met. Subcultures of some radical, ethnic and religious groups influence the process of aging, specifically, the status and treatment of the elderly. Subculture factors can influence the life chances and lifestyles of the elderly, especially if there is a significant intergenerational cultural gap between aging parents and their children or grandchildren.

## Health

Marshall (1993) proposes that the majority of people retain adequate levels of health until well into their later years. Severe health problems may lead to institutionalization, but as Verena Haldemann and Andrew Wister point out, approximately seven percent of people over age 65 are institutionalized. Even among people aged 85 and older, only 39 percent live in institutionalized settings. The typical older person lives in a home-like setting in the community. Over half of these community-dwelling elderly, if they are over age 65, will experience some permanent limitation of their major activities, although they may require only limited assistance.

In Chappell's Activities of Daily Living Inventory (1999), she describes that approximately ten percent of respondents over age 65 may require assistance with any one item on the inventory. The people who need help with at least one-item rises to about 30 to 50 percent among people 85 and older. Chappell (1999) suggests:

> ...The vast majority of older people are in fact reasonably independent, with only a minority being severely ill and thus limited in their independence. (Victoria Times Colonist, Monday May 10, 1999, p. A-6)

Marshall (1993) indicates that of the most damaging stereotypes about old age is the view that aging is associated naturally with illness and physical decline. This is a stereotype widely shared by young people, who greatly overestimate the proportion of older people who live in institutions. It is also a stereotype shared by many aged people who are more sedentary than they need to be, as they believe it is inappropriate or dangerous to be physically active. The medical and health professions often reinforce this stereotype. In the research by Pierre Ouellette he discovers a high level of passive leisure activity in older people. Fortunately, cultural expectations are changing. Some older people feel their level of activity and independence decreasing as they age. There is concern whether certain activity patterns are appropriate in later life. In the context of family, we see delicate negotiation between elderly parents and their adult children. The adult children attempt to provide appropriate security and assistance to their parents without creating or reinforcing dependency. The general ambivalence in this area is apparent in our western culture. For example, in many movies, adults are portrayed as if they lived their entire lives without parents playing any role. Also, if older persons are included as characters, they are portrayed as dependent or as interference in the lives of their adult children.

Marshall (1993) prompts concerns about independence versus dependency are likely to become more prevalent simply because of the extension of life expectancy. Marshall (1993) suggests as death itself is postponed, morbidity and functional limitations are not postponed to the same extent. He suggests:

> ...As deaths from cardiological causes are decreasing, we cannot delay the onset of osteoporosis, vision difficulties, and many other physical conditions, which make the older person at least partially dependent on others. (p. 7)

## On change

This literature review covers relevant information on change theory and transition from key authors. A description of change, transitions, phases of transitions, principles for successful transitions, impacts of change in one's world and seeing life as a system are included in the review.

A majority of authors describe change as an external circumstance, a situation or an event. Transition is difficult to handle, not change. Transition involves internal the psychological processing of information and experiences as individuals come to terms with the new situation. Change occurs quickly while transition occurs slowly. People are said to resist change, but more often it is the transition they are resisting. They fear loss of identity, disorientation and potential for failure in the new world. Common reactions to change affect the physical, emotional, intellectual and spiritual lives of people. (Bridges, 1993) Survival depends not so much on what happens but on how people handle what happens. (Pritchett, 1992)

## Phases of Transition

Bridges (1993) describes three phases of transition: the endings, the neutral zone and the new beginnings. The endings are noted as a time of loss, letting go, getting closure or saying good-bye. As quoted in Bridges (1993) Anatole France, a French writer once said " All changes, even the most longed for, have their melancholy; for what we leave behind is part of ourselves; we must die to one life before we can enter into another." (p. 20)

The first phase of change begins with the endings. Bridges (1993) believes it is important for individuals to accept the reality of losses, as over reaction to change often stems from old losses that have not been dealt with adequately. This over reaction is known as "a transition deficit." To overcome this deficit, individuals need to acknowledge their losses and take the time and personal space for grieving. In the end, by compensating for these losses, one can ease the pain of change. Even the most beneficial change can be ruined if this principle of compensation is overlooked. Individuals should also mark their endings and define what is and what is not occurring for them, otherwise confusion can surface. In <u>Making Sense of Life's Changes - Transitions - Strategies for coping with the difficult, painful, and confusing times in your life,</u> William Bridges suggests:

> The ending-then-beginning pattern represents the way a person changes and grows, and although one may not want to think about larger issues while in the immediate turmoil of transition, they must finally be dealt with if one is to understand not only what is happening but why, when, and how it is happening. (p. 22)

Individuals must consider the bigger picture and think about their direction and where they are destined to go.

Bridges (1993) describes the second phase of transition as the neutral zone. In this "zone" individuals are in-between time, in chaos or in the wilderness. This is where anxiety rises and motivation falls. Employees miss days of work while old wounds resurface and feelings of being overloaded overwhelm them. Left unmanaged, these feelings can lead the person to chaos. Bridges also suggests that these disorganized and tired people respond halfheartedly to any competition or demands in the workplace. They may even sabotage their organization or themselves. But the neutral zone is also a time for creativity. People can take advantage of this zone by capitalizing on its confusion and opportunity to foster innovation. This is a time to step back, take stock, reflect and try new things, a time to create more adaptive and effective ways of solving problems and developing discussions.

Many people do not understand this zone because it involves a journey. This journey takes time to unfold and develop. During this time of uncertainty people often begin to play follow the leader because they do not know where they are going and feel uncomfortable and anxious. If they see someone who looks like she knows where she is going, they follow her. This stage requires time and reflection for reorientation and redefinition. It is also a time when turnover can occur in an organization and when temporary sources of support and control are required.

Bridges (1993) pictures the third phase in transition as the new beginnings. It is a time of being with it, a new chapter or renewal. The old way was fine for the world that is now gone, but now a new chapter is needed for each new day. Quite often, a successful transition takes time. A painful crisis can lead people into new levels of energy and focus. Such renewal requires time for reflection on attitudes and ideas as well as time for the prioritization and organization of activities and commitments to keep moving forward. People move through transition at different speeds. Transition is a time for self-reliance. Unfortunately, most people have a transition deficit. They have not had adequate time to complete their transition cycle before the next change strikes. Peter Senge et al suggests, "We often spend so much time coping with problems along our path that we only have a dim or even inaccurate view of what's really important to us." AI and the Quest - The Quote Center (1990).

In Leading Change, Kotter (1996) characterizes an eight-stage process for creating major change. The stages he suggests are establishing a sense of urgency; creating the guiding coalition; developing a vision and strategy; communicating the change vision; empowering broad-based action; generating short-term wins; consolidating gains and producing more change; and anchoring new approaches in the culture. These stages are based on the fundamental insight that major change will not happen easily. Kotter suggests that:

> Needed change can still stall because of inwardly focused cultures, paralyzing bureaucracy, parochial politics, a low level of trust, lack of teamwork, arrogant attitudes, a lack of leadership in middle management, and the general fear of the unknown. (p. 20)

In Leading Organizational Change and Transitions Workshop, Martin (1999) describes the work of R. Herschowitz and H. Levinson. These writers suggest four stages of change including the impact, recoil-turmoil, adjustment and reconstitution. At the onset of change, individuals experience disorientation, anger, daze and shock. These experiences trigger the fight-fright-flight response. In the second phase, people start to search for what has been lost and begin to find a replacement to cope with their current situation. Reactions in this stage include rage, anxiety, depression, guilt and shame. After a period of time, people begin to recover from the negative aspects of the change and move into a more hopeful place. Their attention becomes more focused and proactive as they start to explore new relationships and responsibilities. They spend time testing solutions to problems. In the final reconstitution stage, people relinquish their past and move towards problem-solving tasks for their new situation. Their losses are replaced and new attachments begin to form as they test new strengths and opportunities.

## Exponential possibilities with attitude

Schein (1993) summarizes the work of Kurt Lewin in the following comments:

> Contemporary theories of attitude change
> to be trivial and superficial when applied to

some of the profound changes that the prisoners had undergone, but I found Lewin's basic change model of unfreezing, changing, and refreezing to be a theoretical foundation upon which change theory could be built solidly. The key, of course, was to see that human change, whether at the individual or group level, was a profound psychological dynamic process that involved painful unlearning without loss of ego identity and difficult relearning as one cognitively attempted to restructure one's thoughts, perceptions, feelings, and attitudes. (p. 2)

Schein (1993) describes unfreezing as a "quasi-stationary equilibria" supported by a large force field of driving and restraining forces. In order for change to occur, this force field must be altered under complex psychological conditions. If only a driving force toward change is added, it often produces an immediate counter force to maintain equilibrium. This leads to an important insight. Equilibrium can be moved if restraining forces are removed as driving forces in the system. Equilibrium is hard to get because there are often psychological defenses or group norms embedded within the organizational or community culture.

In order to become motivated to change, people must accept new information and connect it to something they care about. They will experience survival anxiety if they do not change, if they fail to meet their needs or if they fail to achieve other goals or ideals.

The key to effective change management is the ability to balance disconfirming data with psychological safety. When this happens, a person can feel the survival anxiety and still become motivated to change. True artistry of change management lies in the various tactics that change agents employ to create psychological safety, reduce anxiety, create genuine motivation to learn and change.

In refreezing, new behavior becomes congruent with the actions and personality of the learner. If this does not happen, new rounds of disconfirmation can be set off. As a result, a person can unlearn the very things she has learned.

Kurt Lewin was a physicist by training. He knew the laws of scientific inquiry and objectivity. Schein (1993) proposed that:

> For him to have discovered that human systems cannot be treated with that level of objectivity is, therefore, an important insight that is all too often ignored in our change and consultation literature. (p. 8)

## Principles For Successful Transitions

Bridges (1993) says that, to manage transition people must deal with losses. They need to decide what is over in life and what is not. This decision helps one decide what can be replaced, redefined, reinvented, or relinquished. Individuals going through change must explore any and all information that helps them deal effectively with modifications. It is essential that they go through a time of mourning. Then they can take time to locate a symbolic piece of the past to carry into the future. People can keep a positive attitude and focus on the things that are going well in life.

Bridges (1993) also suggests that people can often feel caught between the demands of conflicting systems and end up like immobilized Hamlets trying to decide "to be or not to be." Hamlet as cited in Bridges (p. 34) People can process most of the necessary business of the neutral zone if they feel protected, encouraged and provided with structures and opportunities to move forward. Accordingly, in a successful new beginning, a person must convert the possibilities she discovered in the neutral zone into objectives and, then, laid out a plan. This involves being open to shifts and corrections in the plan as events and experiences occur in life that require modification. People need to try to keep other, unrelated changes from intruding on their attention and energy.

## Impacts of Change

Bridges (1993) suggests that change impacts people personal worlds including their relationships with family members and with people at work and in the community. Pritchett and Pound (1992) share this same thought. They outline ways of handling change. They suggest becoming a change agent to have personal control over one's attitudes. This can make ownership of the changes easier to handle. Pritchett and Pound also suggest that individuals choose battles carefully by being tolerant of other people or management's mistakes. In this time of challenge, a sense of humor may allow for strengths to become weaknesses. In this instance, stress management techniques can be used to process information carefully and invent the future instead of redesigning the past.

In <u>Making Sense of Life's Changes</u>, Bridges describes the following five categories that can bring about changes in people's lives:

Losses of relationships including spouse's death, a friend moving away, marital separations, children leaving home, parting with friends, death of a pet, the loss of an admired hero, or anything that narrows the field of relationships.

Changes in home life such as getting married or having a child; having a spouse retire; becoming ill or recovering from illness; returning to school; changing jobs; going into depression; remodeling or moving into a new home; experiencing domestic tension; or anything that has changed the content or quality of a person's life.

Personal changes such as getting sick or well again; experiencing notable successes or failures; changing sexual activity, eating or sleeping habits; starting or stopping school; changing lifestyle or appearance markedly can have impact.

Work and financial changes such as getting fired; retiring or changing jobs; changes within your organization; increase or decrease in income; taking on new loans or mortgages; discovering that career advancement is blocked can also have impact.

Bridges (1980) suggests inner changes such as spiritual awakening; deepening social or political awareness; psychological insights; changes in self-image or values; the discovery of a new dream or the abandonment of an old one; or simply one of those nameless shifts which causes people to say, "I'm changing." (p. 22)

Thomas Holmes and Richard Rahe compiled a list of these kinds of events as discussed in Bridges

(1980). They worked out a point system to record the relative impact of each event in a person's life. The points range from 100 for the death of a spouse to 11 for a minor violation of the law. Thousands have taken this test, and their scores have been correlated with their health during the ensuing year or two. Results indicate that a score of less than 150 points puts people in the average group with a one out of three chance of experiencing a serious health change in the next two years. If a person's score is 150 to 300 points, their chances of health changes rise to fifty percent. If a person's score is over 300 points, the odds for serious illness in the ensuing two-year period rise to almost nine in ten. No wonder so many people find their situations complicated by illness shortly after retirement. Some endings close out chapters in people's lives and some beginnings open new doors.

## Seeing Life Change as a System

In Seeing Systems, Barry Oshry (1996) writes:

> We spend our lives in systems: in the family, the classroom, the friendship group, the team, the organization, the task force, the church, the community, the bowling league, the nation, the ethnic group. (p. xi)

Oshry (1996) suggests that as members of systems, people have emotional responses such as joy, sadness, exhilaration and despair; good and bad relationships; opportunities and frustrations. However, they are not aware that these experiences are directly related to the systems they are part of. When people do not see where they are in the system, they may not understand others. When they do not understand others they sometimes develop myths and prejudices. They hurt and destroy others. They become strangers when friendships are possible. They oppress others when a life of peace and harmony is possible. "All of this happens without awareness or choice." (p. xii)

When people learn systems thinking, according to Oshry, (1996) they know what life is about. They pay attention to their own part within the system. Even then, however, they can remain unaware of the part they play within the rest of the system. Matters become worse when people think they know what is going on but in actual fact, do not. This 'spatial blindness' becomes a source of considerable misunderstanding and conflict.

People experience life in their own way each day. They do not see complex sets of events in the past as they relate to each present moment. This 'temporal blindness' as described by Oshry (1996) becomes a source of substantial misunderstanding and conflict.

Wheatley and Kellner-Rogers (1999) suggest that a self-organizing world is best understood by investigation of its paradoxes.

> Life, free to create itself, as it will, moves into particular forms, into defined patterns of being. Pathways and habits develop. Over time, these become boundaries, limiting the freedom of self-expression. Who we are become limited as we strive to continue creating a self, and that reference constrains us. This deeply paradoxical self-referential process has intrigued humankind for thousands of years. Early Hindu sages of the Vedic tradition described self-reference as one of the five elements of spiritual practice. Carl Jung noted that the snake with its tail in its mouth - a being consuming itself - is a universal and timeless image" (p. 48)

Wheatley and Kellner-Rogers (1999) believe that the universal process of self-reference exists on all levels of scale. What people see is influenced by who they decide to be. It is interesting to note that information relayed from the outside world through the eye accounts for only 20 percent of what people use to create their perception. At least 80 percent of the information that the brain works with is already inside the brain. People create their own worlds by choosing what to notice.

Change can occur as people take time to reflect on change. People can change personally if they believe change will lead to self-preservation. Change will not occur if people cannot find a place for themselves in a new version of the world. People need to be able to view their suitability in their new world. People can be influenced to change if the information they receive connects with their personal identity. Every act of organization occurs around an identity and every change occurs only if people identify with it. People engage in change only when they discover that they may be more of who they are by becoming something different.

Wheatley and Kellner-Rogers (1999) suggest that evolutionary theories contribute strongly to ideas on change. Charles Darwin began with an assumption that life is a struggle and that change is a defense strategy directly related to struggles with external hostile forces. His assumption can lead to a belief that fear is the primary motivation for change.

Bridges (1993) suggests that transition is a natural process involving disorientation and reorientation. It marks turning points on paths to growth.

> Throughout nature, growth involves periodic accelerations and transformations: Things go slowly for a time and nothing seems to change- until suddenly the

eggshell cracks, the branch blossoms, the
tadpole" tail shrinks away, the leaf falls,
and the bird molts, and the hibernation
begins. (p. 5)

It is the same with human beings, although the
signs are less clear than they are in nature, the
functions of transitions are the same. Change can
lead to key moments in the natural process of self-
renewal.

## Achievement of balance in retirement

This literature review describes basic components
for achievement of balance in retirement. Balance
encompasses what is most important to you, your
mind, body and soul, in order to create a high
level of self-esteem and passion for life. In the
quality of life, this involves participation in
community activities, recreation, volunteer
activities, physical activities, travel, family, life-
long learning, financial planning and goal setting.

The January issue of Chatelaine Magazine (1995)
describes a study of 164 retired people, psychology
researchers at the University of Guelph and
Queen's University in Kingston, Ontario suggest
that contentment depends on many of the same
factors that helped people be happy when they
were working. Retirees need a sense of purpose,
often gained from volunteer work or hobbies.
Maintaining a routine and interacting with other

people, not just family members also contribute to a happy retirement.

McKay (1998) suggests in 1978, the unemployment rate for individuals from 55 to 59 and 60 to 64 was 5.4% and 5.5% respectively. Today, 7.5% of 55 to 59-year-olds and 7.7% of 60 to 64-year-olds are unemployed. While there are older workers out of work, there's also a large number of under-65s who are not in the workforce at all since they are retiring earlier. According to Statistics Canada, the number of Canadians who retired after the age of 64 fell from 50% to 29% between 1980 and 1996. Concurrently, the number of Canadians who retired before the age of 60 grew from 16% to 34%.

McKay (1998) confirms with Victor Marshall, director of the Institute for Human Development, Life Course and Aging at the University of Toronto suggests:

> The issue of age will become increasingly significant. As the population ages, governments will need to re-examine public and social policies. Meanwhile, Canadian businesses will need to look at their own policies and practices to ensure that they, too, are ready to deal with the graying of the workforce. It's my view that the smartest companies will embrace the changes. (p. 73)

Hanisch (1994) confirms with Woodruff-Pak (1988) suggests retirement from work is important in our society because the life expectancy of a 65 year old man and woman is about 80 and 84 years, respectively. If one lives long enough to retire at 65, it is likely that he or she will live another 15 - 20 years in retirement.

Hanisch (1994) confirms that satisfaction and general happiness in retirement are related to good health and income. The research by Scheier and Carver (1985, 1987) indicates that a positive disposition has positive effects on health, which in turn has positive effects on retirement satisfaction. McGoldrick (1983) and Dorfman et al. (1985) report that the perceived quality of retirees' social contacts with family and friends are important to retirees' satisfaction.

Research by Fried et al (1994) confirms with Atchley, an authority on retirement, suggesting that there are three distinct reasons older people retire:

1. They are interested in pursuing other activities.

2. They find it difficult to continue working because of failing health.

3. They are unable to find work.

In the Canadian Press Newswire, Kelloway, (1994) a psychology professor at the University of Guelph. Suggests that planning for a successful retirement involves more than just financial goals and strategies. People are better off when they have a sense of purpose.

> Satisfaction in retirement is connected to the same factors involved in those found at work. That is, having a sense of purpose and contact with people outside the family...it wouldn't hurt at least in the initial period after retirement to have concrete plans as opposed to saying 'well I can travel' or something vague and general. (p. 1)

Kelloway (1994) suggests, while employed, people devote most of their thoughts and energies to their career, not retirement.

> It's hard to imagine retirement...you can imagine a vacation, which is three weeks of not working, but now try to imagine 20 years and it's quite a different matter. (p. 2)

Kelloway's (1994) research suggests people tend to be more satisfied with retirement if they have some kind of activity and interpersonal contacts outside the home as working brings with it structure, such as being at the job at 8 a.m. or eating lunch at noon. Such schedules disappear upon retirement and people must then redraw their daily structure to suit this new way of life. The great shock with retirement is the transition period, especially for those who have always relied on others to make decisions for them. Kelloway (1994) suggests:

> It's not that you don't need structure any longer, you do, but it's one you can plan to suit your life...On one hand there are some people who think they are very much the masters of their own destiny...and there are others who think that everything that happens to them is luck or chance. (p. 2)

Table 1.  Center for Health Promotion Quality of Life Model

Adapted in total from Raphael (1998) <u>Quality of life indicators and health:  Current status and emerging concepts</u>, (p.12)

| Domain | Description | Indicators |
|---|---|---|
| **Being** | "Who one is" | **Physical being** |
| | **Three sub-domains:** | Physical health, exercise and physical appearance |
| | Physical being | **Psychological** |
| | Psychological being | **being** |
| | Spiritual being | Cognition, feelings, self-esteem, Self-concept and self-control |
| | | **Spiritual being** |
| | | Personal values, spiritual values and Standards of conduct |
| **Belonging** | An individual's fit with | **Physical belonging** |
| | their environment | Connections with physical environment |
| | **Three sub-domains:** | of home, work, neighbourhood and school |
| | Physical belonging | and community. |
| | Social belonging | **Social belonging** |
| | Community belonging | Links with social environments involving acceptance by others. |

| Domain | Description | Indicators |
|--------|------------|------------|
| | | **Community belonging** |
| | | Access to resources such as adequate income, services, employment, recreation and community events. |
| Becoming | Purposeful activities | **Practical becoming** |
| | Carried out to express oneself and achieve personal goals, hopes and aspirations | Day-to-day activities. **Leisure becoming** Activities that promote relaxation and reduce stress |
| | **Three sub-domains:** Practical becoming Leisure Becoming Growth becoming | **Growth becoming:** Activities that promote maintenance or improvement of knowledge and skills |

According to Table 1, Rafael (1998) this model focuses on health not illness and views quality of life as a concept not an exclusionary term or measurement. It is a multidimensional approach looking at interrelated aspects of an individual's life. The model also includes the notion of personal control over one's life, which would include personal choices.

There are many people who view retirement as a paid vacation for the rest of their lives. Boulmetis (1997) agrees with Fetridge (1990). Boulmetis (1997) suggests that:

> Somewhere between the sixth and fifteenth month of retirement they begin to wonder what else there is. (p. 15)

Boulmetis (1997) suggests adults who retire often seek new full or part-time careers. Those seeking part-time work are usually trying to make ends meet or hope to fulfill personal needs like contributing to society or the need for social affiliations. Many older adults cannot afford to retire or choose not to do so because the problem of unemployment or underemployment for older workers is overwhelming. To them, the normal difficulties of facing any job seeker are inflated since older workers encounter discriminatory practices, stereotypical attitudes, changes in their abilities and a negative self-image. For a variety of economic, physiological or psychological reasons, people are not ending their careers with retirement. For them, retirement takes them into another career transition that moves them to yet another career cycle.

## Mind

Thursz et al (1995) suggest wellness focuses on self-responsibility and the need for assertiveness in creating the life you want, rather than passive in just reacting to circumstances. Through an emphasis on freedom of choice, wellness approaches increase the responsibility of self-care for individuals. Wellness is essentially am empowering philosophy. It has a goal of helping people identify areas of their lives which they have control, and assists them to make healthy lifestyle choices that enhance their physical and emotional well-being, as well as their continued ability to make even more healthy choices.

At the Center for Health Promotion at the University of Toronto, Raphael et al (1998) designed a model of quality of life that is built upon a focus of health rather than illness. The Center developed the concept of life quality related to the questions: What is life and what is quality of life? The University of Toronto Center for Health Promotion defines their conceptualization of quality of life as:

> ...The degree to which a person enjoys important possibilities in their life. Enjoyment encompasses two meanings: experience of subjective satisfaction and the possession or achievement of some characteristic or state. (p. 12)

The Center for Health Promotion quality of life model reflects three life domains according to Raphael. These domains are identified as that of Being, Belonging and Becoming.

> Being reflects who one is, and has three sub-domains of physical, psychological and spiritual being. The Belonging domain concerns the person's fit with his/her environment and also has three sub-domains. Becoming refers to the purposeful activities carried out to express one and to achieve personal goals, hopes and aspirations. (p. 13)

## Body

Holmes and Rahe (1967) suggest life change has been discussed with regard to general health and adjustment. Relocation's, loss of roles, friends, and spouse, reduced financial resources and changes in physical capacity are all potentially stressful. As stress accumulates, the older individual may lack the resources for coping. Chiriboga and Cutler (1980) suggest the older adult may be more vulnerable to the stress and experience reduced life satisfaction. Within this framework, it is expected that higher levels of recent life changes be related to lower life satisfaction.

Chappell (1998) indicates severe mental declines resulting in cognitive impairment and dementia are not characteristic of the vast majority of seniors. Physical health does decline slowly and gradually throughout life. This decline becomes particularly evident during old age.

> Chronic conditions - not acute infections - are characteristic of old age; chronic conditions are not dealt with well within our medicalized health care system. The non-medical determinants of health are therefore particularly relevant when discussing old age. (p. 89)

Chappell (1998) suggests seniors are knowledgeable about and adhere to a variety of well-established or traditional views on health promotion, such as refraining from smoking, drinking alcohol and or skipping meals.

> However, the adoption of more recent perspectives on health promotion, such as having mammograms and minimizing the use of prescription medications, is more evident in younger populations. This suggests that seniors should be a target group for the dissemination of information in these new areas of health promotion. (p. 90)

Beehr (1986) proposes health is described as an important determinant of individuals' decision to retire. Based on subsequent mortality rates and previous illnesses, Diamond and Hausman (1984) suggest the probability of retirement increases as self-assessed and objective health status declines. Dorfman, Kouhout and Heckert (1985) suggest health as a strong correlate of retirement satisfaction with those retirees that experience health problems more likely to be less satisfied with their retirement than those who do not have health problems. Larson (1978) and O'Brien (1981) suggest that health has also been found to be strongly related to older individuals' well being and a strong predictor of life satisfaction or general happiness. In addition Riddick and Daniel (1984) suggest as health problems increase, participation in leisure activities has been found to decrease.

McNamara (1999) indicates, as the population ages, more people are diagnosed with Alzheimer's disease. The risk of getting this disease increases with age. Only 3% of women between the ages of 65 to 74 have Alzheimer's disease compared to the 47% of women over the age of 85 who are at greatest risk for this dreaded disease. Alzheimer's disease appears to be a disease of oxidation. Free radical damage destroys the nerve cells of the brain. The brain literally shrivels and becomes less functional. McNamara (1999) suggests:

> Antioxidants, such as vitamin E, have been shown to slow the progression of this disease better than the prescription drug selegiline. Antioxidants and anti-inflammatory medications protect against

brain cell damage by blocking oxidation. Estrogen also seems to have a positive effect on the disease because estrogen allows for a greater blood flow to tissues, and because estrogen appears to have antioxidant properties. (p.12) Although vitamins, minerals and nutrients such as grape seed extract do most of the following better, estrogen also appears to: improve blood flow to the brain; enhance production of neurotransmitters (brain chemicals such as acetylcholine); block the degradation of neurotransmitters; protect against apoptosis (programmed cell death) of neurons; stimulate brain growth factors and nerve connections; reduce the levels of apolipoprotein E which is a main ingredient of the brain plaque deposits found in Alzheimer's disease. (p. 13)

McNamara (1999) suggests women at greatest risk for developing Alzheimer's disease are those with a parent with the disease, those not taking estrogen replacement, and those not taking a full-range of quality antioxidant vitamin, minerals and essential fatty acids, such as flax seed oil. Essential fatty acids help restore the normal fats to the brain that are damaged in the process of the development of Alzheimer's disease.

McNamara (1999) also suggests that osteoporosis is one of the top ten causes of death in developed countries. If bones become weak, they cannot support the normal stresses demanded by the body and its movements against gravity. The vertebral column compresses under weight of the upper body, and a woman may lose several inches in height within a few years after menopause. The hip joint may fracture necessitating prolonged bed rest. This may be complicated by a fatal episode of pneumonia or thromboembolism, which is the formation of blood clots that dislodge and clog the heart or lungs.

Marshall (1993) advises:

> ...Physical activity is an increasingly important leisure pursuit for the elderly, but by no means the only one. The elderly are posing new demands on the educational system and creating new organizations for recreational, tourist, and sedentary leisure pursuits. (p. 5)

## Soul

Sobel (1991) submits many of us look to retirement for the well-deserved, uninterrupted leisure we've been craving through all these working years - a time to be free of structure and pressure. After devoting a lifetime to studying the nature of enjoyment, a professor of psychology and education at the University of Chicago, Csikszentmihalyi suggests if we expect to truly enjoy retirement - it has to be more like work than play. Sobel (1991) suggests:

> Retirement activities have to be challenging to be satisfying. Puttering around the garden or idly picking up a book is not going to be enough. The things that make people happy are goals and challenges that let them hone their skills or develop new ones. (p.72)

Frankl (1963, 1978) alludes that lack of purpose in life is manifested in boredom. People who are bored do not experience a feeling of purpose in their lives. The most successful retirement plans involve taking a new approach to life rather than retreating from it. This includes volunteering for churches, hospitals or schools; starting a new business, developing an elaborate hobby such as boat building or expanding one's desire for knowledge through furthering one's educational pursuits. As discussed by Csikszentmihalyi in Sobel (1991), he suggests these activities become successful if they produce a feeling of flow or a state of total concentration and utter enjoyment that makes life worth living. It is the artist in the throes of creation, the surgeon in the operating theater, and the rock climber on the face of the mountain experience.

Sobel (1991) suggests:

> Flow is how you feel when you are
> completely engaged by what you are doing,
> with no distressing self-consciousness, no
> sense of time. Worries tend to leave your
> mind. You feel very much alive. Flow is a
> delicate balance between the challenge
> inherent in an activity and the skill you
> bring to that task. If there is too much
> challenge relative to skill then you feel
> anxiety, not flow. When a challenge is too
> small for your skills, you feel bored. (p. 72)

Sobel (1991) suggests the more time a person
spends in flow during the week, the better the
overall quality of his/her reported experience.
People who are more often in flow are especially
likely to feel strong, active, creative, concentrated
and motivated. Flow can be found in some
unlikely situations such as ironing or even
washing dishes. The mental approach to such
tasks invite flow as an invitation to whatever
challenge might be there and striving to meet it.
Am I doing this as well as possible? How could I
improve my performance? There are no rules for
washing dishes, but if you want to enjoy these
activities, you can create your own rules.

Volunteering as discussed by Foot (1996) is an
important part of the Canadian economic profile.
As we are moving toward the turn of the century,
the well educated, aging baby-boomer generation

will be turning to volunteering to round out their lives and to meet their altruistic desires. This will be a tremendous advantage to non-profit societies and organizations in both areas of available human resource and financial contribution.

Foot (1996) states that the baby boomers will come to the rescue of non-profit organizations. At the same time as governments are withdrawing financial support, organizations are becoming more complicated and complex to run. As this occurs in organizations, the experienced baby boomers are seeking meaningful work outside of the paid workplaces. Foot contends these people are interested in giving their knowledge and skills to volunteering, in return, for the satisfaction found in the altruism of volunteering.

Thursz et al (1995) recommends a useful visual model of a wheel of wellness. It is useful in helping older persons visually experience a sense of empowerment as a holistic model for wellness and prevention. Spirituality is the core of the wheel and one of five major life tasks that empirical data support as important. The four additional tasks are self-regulation, work, love and friendship.

Thursz et al (1995) proposes this model incorporates research and theoretical concepts from a variety of disciplines, including anthropology, education, medicine, psychology, religion and sociology. It provides an integrated paradigm that can serve as a basis for theory building, clinical interventions, education, advocacy and conscious raising. The five life tasks exemplify the characteristics of a healthy person and interact dynamically with several life forces: family, community, religion, education, government, media and business/industry. The life force and life tasks interact with and are affected by global events, natural and human, positive as well as negative.

Thursz et al (1995) suggests in a healthy person, all life tasks are interconnected and interact for the well being or detriment of the individual. Persons planning wellness interventions must conduct needs assessments and design interventions to address holistic functioning in each area identified.

Thursz et al (1995) alludes what is seen as disempowered and unhealthy in one society may be viewed as both healthy and desirable from other cultural perspectives. In Buddhist cultures, for example, emotional detachment from life is viewed as desirable, even a state of advancement to a higher level of functioning. Within these cultures, detachment is a sign of healthy functioning. In Western societies, the same behaviors would usually be viewed as unhealthy and a sign of the beginning of a social breakdown cycle.

Thursz et al (1995) suggests empowerment of older people is defined differently in different cultures. Empowerment as defined by Western cultures could actually be counterproductive in Eastern cultures. Empowerment from a wellness perspective, a viable concept in Western society, may be useful regardless of culture so long as cultural definitions of wellness behaviors are used as a basis for implementing wellness interventions.

Furthermore Thursz et al (1995) suggests attention, physical, emotional and spiritual wellness seem to be universal aspects of all cultures. Older persons who experience wellness are, by definition, those who meet the highest standard and expectations of the culture in which they live. They are able to experience a sense of empowerment regardless of their circumstances. A cross-cultural perspective on individual psychological empowerment may best be achieved through a wellness philosophy. Social breakdown may occur in all societies; however, the definition of the stages and preconditions may vary considerably. Clearly, all societies need to examine healthy roles and behaviors of older people, and to foster these roles in order to enhance the quality of life for persons across the life span.

## Financial Planning

Fried et al (1994) submits most people look forward to retirement, although attitudes toward retirement seem to be closely linked to finances. People who expect to be comfortable financially tend to look forward to retirement. People who are dissatisfied with their work lives may also look forward to retirement, although their lack of financial resources may create some dread concerning a decline in income following the loss of a paycheck. The process of retirement begins years before people actually retire from their jobs. Effective retirement planning needs to begin early in adulthood. Unfortunately, many people are faced with various financial pressures such as mortgages and their children's college education during the same years in which they should be saving and investing for retirement. For people who fail to plan for retirement, Social Security may be their only source of income. For many of these people, Social Security fails to cover all of their needs.

In a series of studies on mental health and retirement, Kelloway (1994) and co-author Julian Barling, professor in the psychology department of Queen's University in Kingston, found that finances don't predict happiness as much as other factors.

> This leads me to believe that employers have a bad habit in Canada of offering only financial planning seminars to prospective

> retirees...But as retirement approaches,
> people have to think about what they are
> going to do with this time... it is the people
> who get involved and have a sense that
> they are in control of their affairs who tend
> to take an active part in planning their
> retirement. (p. 1)

Kelloway (1994) proposes some people will believe
they have handled their retirement planning if
they have a company pension and Canada
Pension Plan as someone else is taking care of
things for them, while other people will get
actively involved in their own retirement by
planning through RRSPs, insuring they have an
income and not relying on those external supports
so much. The same thoughts apply for planning
quality in their lives. People who plan their lives
will probably have a more satisfactory retirement
because they are motivated and in control of their
own destiny.

In North America, according to the U.S.
Department of Labor, only three out of every one
hundred Americans reach age sixty-five with any
degree of financial security. Ninety-seven out of
one hundred Americans who are sixty-five and
over must depend on their monthly Social
Security checks to survive. Waitley (1996)
suggests:

> ...It is more difficult to survive and thrive
> in a global economy fraught with constant

change, instability and the rising
expectations of developing nations. Only
five out of every 100 Americans who are in
the higher income professions such as law
and medicine, reach 65 without having to
depend on Social Security. So few
individuals achieve any degree of financial
success, regardless of their level of income
during their most productive years. (p. 2)

Waitley (1996) suggests:

Most people apparently live their lives
under the delusion that they are
immortal...they squander their money,
their time and their minds with activities
that are tension relieving instead of goal-
achieving. Most people work to get through
the week with enough money to spend on
the weekend... and hope that the winds of
fate blow them into some rich and
mysterious port of call. They look forward
to when they can retire someday in the
distant future, and live on Fantasy Island
somewhere. (p.3)

What kind of asset allocation should retirees end
up with as they near retirement? Cullen (1998)
suggests the answer depends largely on individual
factors and a key one is risk tolerance. The more
aggressive and stock-heavy a portfolio, the more

growth it should provide over time; but remember that as one enters retirement, there is less time to wait out market fluctuations, so there is a real danger in keeping too much money in stocks. Cullen (1998) suggests turning to a financial advisor for more in-depth help or starting with these two websites: Standard and Poor's (www.personalwealth.com) and Quicken (www.quicken.com) both viewed in 2000.

## Lessons in Goal-Setting

Waitley (1996) suggests that specific goals are crucial to successful goal setting. He defines *"SMART"* or *Specific, Measurable, Achievable, Real and Time-based* by Hyrum Smith, chairman and cofounder of Franklin Quest Company. Waitley (1996) suggests specific goals are crucial, as the brain cannot handle vague directions. *"Specific"* goals assist the brain to visualize more clearly. This visualization becomes a critical factor in success. *"Measurable"* goals provide a clear outcome focusing on a destination point. By stating goals with specific numbers and targets, one can realistically determine the outcome of their actions and then determine appropriate changes in order to meet their targets. Waitley (1996) proposes that goals must be *"achievable, real"* and stretches one's limits to aim high, and lofty enough to inspire hard work, yet realistic enough to provide solid hope for attainment. These goals should be set within a realistic, specific and doable *"time"* frame providing a target to aim towards. Waitley (1996) recommends the use of positive affirmation statements to reinforce one's goals using the pronoun *"I"* and other action modifiers that convey emotions such as happily or enthusiastically. Waitley (1996) advises keeping goal statements short and concise using terms that imply the goals have been attained. Waitley (1996) also suggests keeping goals noncompetitive and avoiding comparisons with others remembering the need to break down goals into smaller components. Waitley (1996) hints the real secret of goal achievement as commitment.

## Self-worth

Waitley (1996) suggests peoples greatest regrets in life are the things they fail to do and advises people not to wait for certainty, as plans are not set in stone. He recommends that plans must be flexible and feels the majority of people never achieve their goals because they fail to plan and, if they fail, they give up or fail to plan again. Waitley (1996) states:

> Aristotle once devised a formula for success and happiness. First, he wrote, ...have a definite, practical idea - a goal or objective. Then he said, adjust all your means to that end. (p. 17)

Waitley (1996) gives credence to what Edgar Mitchell, an astronaut on the Apollo 14 moon mission and founder of the Institute for Noetic Sciences, discovered about goal setting. Edgar Mitchell said:

> I used to say, Gee, I'll be happy when I've done this, but when I got to that point, I found I never was. I discovered that it is the process of doing it that one has to find fulfilling. That is where the happiness is. While it is important to create worthwhile goals, it is equally important to remember

that life is really about the journey you take
toward accomplishing your goals. (p.17)

Waitley (1996) advises people to consider their
strategies, giving equal time to their quality of life
and standard of living, and he believes there is a
distinct difference between the two. Recognizing
this distinction and taking time from the urgent,
to give to the important, is a key component to
life, living in balance and harmony.

# CHAPTER THREE - RESEARCH FINDINGS

## Findings

After the interviews were transcribed and upon reflection one theme, which evolved, were common responses with the group of participants retired over five years. The literature review also suggested some important life transitions in this group as well. The three groups, which evolved out of this study, were:

- Participants considering retirement

- Participants retired less than five years

- Participants retired over five years

The researcher with a view to identify trends analyzed the one-on-one interview and focus group notes and transcripts or patterns in the language or concepts used either within individual participants. As qualitative research in particular relies on the words of participants and the observations of the researcher to express reality, the information gained from these one-on-one interviews and focus group assisted the researcher in developing new and creative approaches to retirement transition based on the words of those considering retirement, and in retirement transition. Our principle data-gathering tool during and after the interviews was the conversation. Kvale (1996) puts the qualitative interview in a context with which we feel harmony, when he states, "Interviews are conversations where the outcome is a coproduction of the interviewer and the subject." (p.xvii)

The participants seemed comfortable with the interview process and the use of the tape recorder. They appreciated the depth of questions. All seemed to enjoy the process and provided thorough and insightful answers to the interview questions. They enjoyed the preamble to each section of questions as it prepared their minds for thinking on each section. Participants in the focus group did not want to leave the session. Some of the things they said were:

> Your questions are good in that they make you think. What are you going to do with your time when you've got all this time on your hands? And I've been thinking about it. And now I can delve deeper into this perhaps.

> I found it quite interesting and very enlightening.

> You have given me more things to think about in retirement. This is very good for me, as I know I will miss my job very much.

## Participant Demographics

A total of thirty participants were interviewed with twenty-seven one-on-one interviews and one focus group with three participants. All of the participants lived on Vancouver Island except for two people, one person lived in Cold Lake, Alberta and the other person lived in Vancouver.

The researcher conducted seven interviews with participants considering retirement. Out of these seven participants there were four females aged 57, 58, 56 and 55 years, two of which worked as teachers, one dietician and one electrical manager; and the three males, two aged 60 years and one 55 years of age, two worked as engineers and one worked as a manager from the forest industry. These participants were all of middle class financial status.

Fifteen interviews were conducted with participants retired less than five years. This included one focus group with three male participants retired less than five years. These participants ranged from 50 to 55 years of age, had worked in the logging industry and were of middle class financial status. It also included twelve one-on-one interviews with eight females aged 57 to 60 years of which four had worked as teachers, two nurses, one nurse's aid and one worked in food services. Also included were four males aged 57 to 60 years, where two worked as teachers, one mill right and one telecommunications technician. These participants were all of middle class financial status.

Eight interviews were conducted with participants who had been retired longer than five years. This included two females aged 70 and 97 years who worked at home raising their children. It also included six male participants ageing from 65 to 97 years of which three worked in the pulp mill industry, two worked as teachers and one worked as an undercover agent or spy.

Based on the review of literature, questions were designed to accommodate the various major topics of retirement. As discussed earlier, these major topics included:

- Change
- The achievement of balance in retirement
- Stages of aging
- The history of retirement

## QUESTIONS FOR PEOPLE WHO ARE JUST CONSIDERING RETIREMENT

### For Focus Groups or Interviews

### On Change

**The following questions are focused on change and transition:**

Why are you now considering retirement?

What do you most look forward to regarding your own retirement?

When did you start planning for retirement?

Where do you see yourself going in retirement?

How might your retirement be affected by your health?

How might family roles change in relation to your retirement?

How can you prepare yourself for retirement?

On a scale from 1 - 5 (1 being low or poor and 5 being high or excellent) how would you rate how you handle change?

## Achievement of Balance in Retirement

### The following questions are focused on the achievement of balance:

In what ways will your life be different from when you were employed?

Describe how you create your life to nurture your physical being through physical health, exercise and physical appearance?

Describe how you create your life to nurture your psychological being through feelings and how you feel about yourself?

Describe how you create your life to nurture your spiritual being through personal values, spiritual values and standards of conduct?

During your transition to retirement, how will you create psychological safety to reduce anxiety and create motivation?

How do you view retirement?

How do you view your retirement goals?

On a scale from 1 - 5 (1 being low or poor and 5 being high or excellent) how would you rate your personal achievement of balance in your life?

## Stages of Aging

## The following questions are focused on the stages of aging:

What is old age?

What is important to you as you approach old age?

What are your expectations for changes in health and longevity?

Describe the problems associated with living on a fixed income.

On a scale from 1 - 5 (1 being low or poor and 5 being high or excellent) how would you rate your level of independence?

## History of Retirement

## The following questions are focused on the history of retirement:

What is retirement?

Why are you now considering retirement?

Do you think you will want to continue to work past the age of 65? Why or why not?

What strategies would you recommend to people who are starting to plan for retirement?

How do you feel about retirement?

On a scale from 1 - 5 (1 being low or poor and 5 being high or excellent) how would you rate your attitude towards retirement?

## QUESTIONS FOR PEOPLE WHO ARE RETIRED, FOR EITHER FOCUS GROUPS OR INTERVIEWS

### On Change

### The following questions are focused on change and transition:

How long have you been retired?

What do you like most about retirement?

What do you like least about retirement?

When did you start planning for retirement?

How has your retirement affected your relationships with family and friends?

Has your retirement been affected by your health?

What advice would you give to people now considering retirement?

On a scale from 1 - 5 (1 being low or poor and 5 being high or excellent) how would you rate how you handle change?

## Achievement of Balance in Retirement

**The following questions are focused on the achievement of balance:**

In what ways is your life different from when you were employed?

Describe how you create your life to nurture your physical being through physical health, exercise and physical appearance?

Describe how you create your life to nurture your psychological being through feelings and how you feel about yourself?

Describe how you create your life to nurture your spiritual being through personal values, spiritual values and standards of conduct?

In your retirement, how do you create psychological safety to reduce anxiety and create motivation?

How do you view retirement?

How do you view your retirement goals?

On a scale from 1 - 5 (1 being low or poor and 5 being high or excellent) how would you rate your personal achievement of balance in your life?

## Stages of Aging

**The following questions are focused on the stages of aging:**

What is old age?

What is important to you as you approach old age?

What are your expectations for changes in health and longevity?

Describe the problems associated with living on a fixed income.

On a scale from 1 - 5 (1 being low or poor and 5 being high or excellent) how would you rate your level of independence?

## History of Retirement

**The following questions are focused on the history of retirement:**

What is retirement?

Why did you retire?

Do you think you will want to continue to work past the age of 65? Why or why not?

What strategies would you recommend to people who are starting to plan for retirement?

How do you feel about retirement?

On a scale from 1 - 5 (1 being low or poor and 5 being high or excellent) how would you rate your attitude towards retirement?

## Responses to questions as viewed by the participants

Results from the questions asked during the interviews are summarized under these major topics of retirement and are discussed below in the findings of participant responses.

## FINDINGS ON CHANGE AS VIEWED BY THE PARTICIPANTS

Persons planning to retire viewed change from the perspective of leaving work for a variety of reasons while persons who had retired found change more difficult to cope with as time evolved.

**Question:** **On a scale from one to five, one being low or poor, and five being high or excellent, how would you rate how you handle change?**

Responses are depicted below in Graph 3.0

- Considering Retirement: average response at 4.8

- Retired less than five years: average response at 3.5

- Retired over five years: average response at 3.0

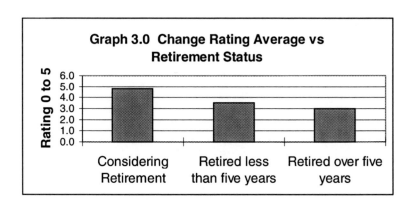

## Question:  Why are you now considering retirement?

As depicted below in Graph 3.1 responses from participants considering retirement varied as follows:

- 29% said that it was time to retire because of their age, as they had worked long enough and it was time to do something different.

- 14% felt their stress at work had mounted and so they felt it was time to do something different rather than work for someone.

- 43% had some health issues, felt they had slowed down and were not physically as strong as they were in their younger years.

- 14% said the incentive of a buy-out package was a nice way to start considering retirement.

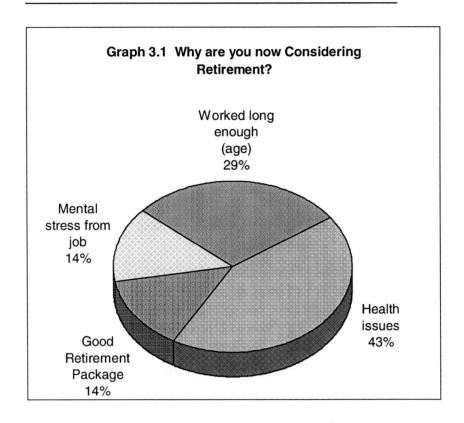

**Graph 3.1  Why are you now Considering Retirement?**

Worked long enough (age) 29%

Mental stress from job 14%

Health issues 43%

Good Retirement Package 14%

## Question:  What do you most like about retirement?

Responses from retired participants were unanimous.

• 100% all agreed that flexibility of time, freedom from schedules to do the things they wanted to do when they wanted to do them was most enjoyed in retirement.  This newfound freedom included time for reflection, hobbies, sports, crafts and spontaneous playtime.

## Question:  What do you least like about retirement?

Responses from retired participants were equally split.

- 50% said there was nothing they disliked about retirement.
- 50% said that time tended to drag on a bit for them in retirement as they missed their working peers, work, paycheck and the structure of the work environment.

## Question:  What do you most look forward to regarding your own retirement?

Responses from participants considering retirement were unanimous.

- All participants said time; freedom from schedules to do the things they wanted to do when they wanted to do it was a luxury of retirement.

## Question: When did you start planning for retirement?

Responses from retired participants varied and are depicted below in Graph 3.2

- 71% said they started to think of the financial aspects of retirement anywhere from 5 to 15 years prior to retirement. They saved money in RRSP's, or with the company plan, and added on additional money when it was available.

- It is interesting to note that 29% said they did not start to think or plan for retirement until a couple of months prior to retirement.

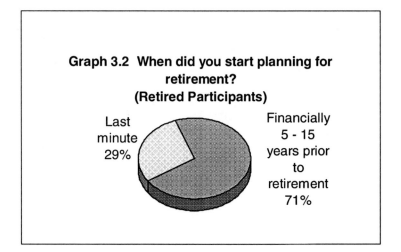

**Graph 3.2 When did you start planning for retirement?**
**(Retired Participants)**

Last minute 29%

Financially 5 - 15 years prior to retirement 71%

## Question:  Where do you see yourself going in retirement?

Responses from participants considering retirement were unanimous.

- All said they initially wanted to just relax and not do anything.  After this initial rest period, they wanted to then have more fun, travel and explore new hobbies or crafts.

## Question:  How might your retirement be affected by your health?

Health is the most important factor when considering retirement and during retirement. Responses from participants considering retirement showed that their health was a very important factor to them in retirement.  This is depicted below in Graph 3.3

- 57% said they were currently in reasonable good health, blessed with good genes.  If they got ill, their retirement would definitely be affected.

- 43% said health had already affected their life and this was traumatic.

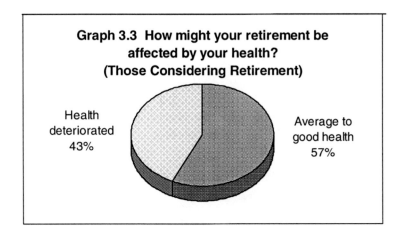

**Graph 3.3 How might your retirement be affected by your health? (Those Considering Retirement)**

Health deteriorated 43%

Average to good health 57%

## Question: Has your retirement been affected by your health?

Responses from retired participants also revealed that health was a very important factor to them in retirement. This is depicted below in Graph 4.4

- 60% of participants who were retired less than five years reported that their health had stayed basically the same. They were healthy before they retired and were currently healthy in retirement.

- 25% of participants who were retired less than five years reported that their health had improved since retirement. They either had time to rest, exercise, prepare meals for good eating or mentioned that they were taking nutritional supplements.

- 15% of participants who were retired over five years reported that their health had deteriorated.

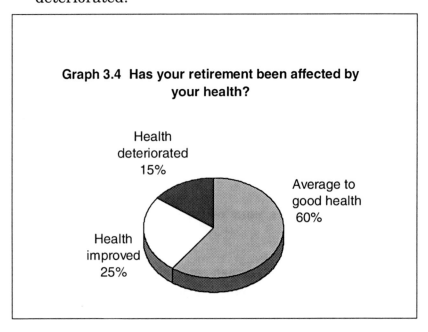

**Graph 3.4  Has your retirement been affected by your health?**

Health deteriorated 15%

Average to good health 60%

Health improved 25%

**Question:  How might family roles change in relation to your retirement?**

Maintaining relationships were viewed as the second most important aspect in retirement. Responses from participants considering retirement show the importance of maintaining relationships.  This is depicted below in Graph 3.5

- 86% thought there was not much change to consider for family roles.  They felt there was more opportunity for involvement with their friends, relatives and immediate families.

- 14% felt that family roles would probably be the same; although they were concerned they would feel they were *"under their spouse's feet."*

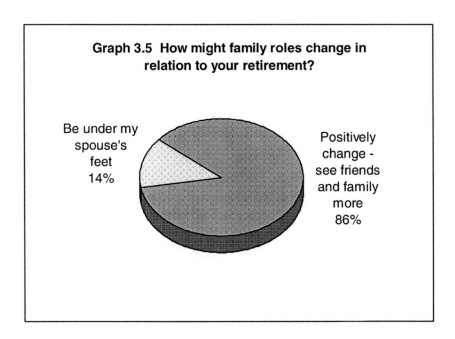

Graph 3.5  How might family roles change in relation to your retirement?

Be under my spouse's feet
14%

Positively change - see friends and family more
86%

**Question:  How has your retirement affected your relationship with family and friends?**

Responses from retired participants emphasized the importance of maintaining close relationships and family bonds.  This is depicted below in Graph 3.6

- 50% said retirement had positively affected their relationships with family as they had more available time to visit with friends, family and relatives.

- 50% reported that retirement had negatively affected their relationship with friends as some friends had moved away from where they worked, so they missed their friends. Others said their friends were still busy working, so they did not see them, or they were working shift work and it was difficult to know when to call on them.

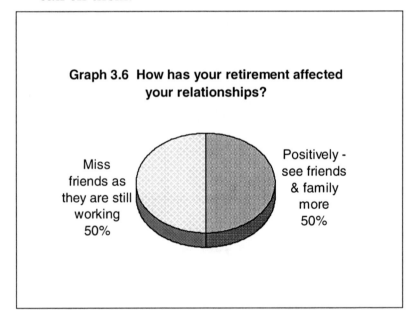

**Graph 3.6  How has your retirement affected your relationships?**

Miss friends as they are still working 50%

Positively - see friends & family more 50%

<u>**Question:**</u> **How can you prepare yourself for retirement?**

Responses from participants considering retirement were varied. This is depicted below in Graph 3.7

- 14% said they started writing some financial, physical, spiritual or psychological goals.

- 43% said they had attended retirement workshops, talked to retired people or had read books.

- 29% said they had financial concerns.

- 14% said they really did not know, as they had never been through retirement before. They just assumed things and worked towards retirement, and if things turned out the way they wanted them to, great, if not, then they would have to change something. They felt they needed to be very flexible about things and do some financial planning.

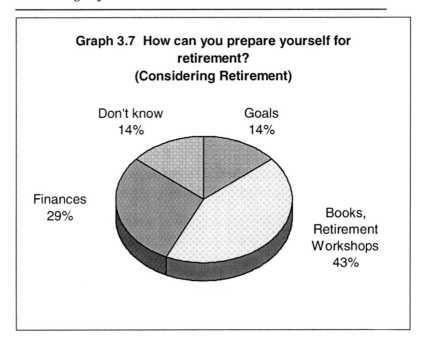

Graph 3.7 How can you prepare yourself for retirement? (Considering Retirement)

Don't know 14%

Goals 14%

Finances 29%

Books, Retirement Workshops 43%

**Question:** **What advice would you give to people now considering retirement?**

Responses from retired participants were wide-ranging.

- Do not give up life for the sake of retirement. Continue to spend for your pleasures, your spouse's pleasures and your children's activities.

- If you feel you currently have a very involved or stressful job, consider weaning away from the job going into another less stressful job if you can.

- Retire as soon as you can, while you have your health, and go out and enjoy retirement.

- If you dislike your job, retire.

- Do not retire if you really enjoy your job.

- Clear up any financial commitments prior to retirement because retirement is a precious time in one's life, and you do not want to deal with on-going payments.

- Sit down with your spouse and find out how much money you need to live by.

- Find out what you will be receiving or what you have in your company pension, Canada Pension Plan, Old Age Pension, RRSP's and any other investments. Find out what your taxes will be the first year so you will not be surprised. Prepare to plan financially, even long term.

- Start to develop hobbies and outside interests now while you are working, well before you retire and incorporate this balance into your life. Remember who you are as a person. You are not only the job you do. Try not to have your whole personal identity tied up in your job.

## FINDINGS ON THE ACHIEVEMENT OF BALANCE IN RETIREMENT AS VIEWED BY THE PARTICIPANTS

**Question:** **In what ways will your life be different from when you were employed?**

Responses from participants considering retirement were split.

- 43% said they would definitely have less money and were concerned about this.

- 57% said they were not worried about money in their retirement.

- All 100% of participants said they needed to establish a routine because they enjoyed some structure, although they also enjoyed their time to be more creative. They felt they needed to have these kinds of boundaries to give them a sense of purpose so they would not lose focus and go all over the place. Yet, in some way they did not want too much structure or routine. This was where it was going to be rather interesting, and they wondered how would they achieve that balance?

- 100% of participants agreed they would have more time for themselves, others, social contacts and social activities. There would be no rush to get to work and less structure during their day, but they would miss their peers from their workplace and would have to find a way of coping with that loss.

**Question:** **In what ways is your life different from when you were employed?**

Responses from retired participants were similar.

- All of the participants agreed they had more time for themselves, others, volunteer groups, social contacts and social activities. There was no rush to get up early in the morning.

- 50% missed their work peers, work structure, mental stimulation and paycheck.

**Question:** **Describe how you create your life to nurture your physical being through physical health, exercise and physical appearance.**

Responses from participants considering retirement were similar, noting that physical activities were important to all. This is depicted below in Graph 3.8

- 71% said that sports such as biking, gardening, walking, golfing and skiing were activities they would continue to partake in.

- 29% said they dyed their hair and loved to take soothing baths. These made them feel better about their self-image.

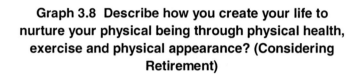

**Graph 3.8 Describe how you create your life to nurture your physical being through physical health, exercise and physical appearance? (Considering Retirement)**

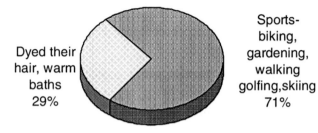

Dyed their hair, warm baths
29%

Sports-biking, gardening, walking golfing,skiing
71%

**Question:** **Describe how you create your life to nurture your psychological being through feelings and how you feel about yourself.**

Responses from participants considering retirement were varied. This is depicted below in Graph 3.9

- 29% said they thought of themselves as a whole person rather than separate parts. When they physically felt well, then spiritually and emotionally everything felt fine. They always had at least one focus per day. This type of focus was self-nurturing, as it provided something to live for, which was very important. They got very excited about life when they took the time to meditate or practice Tai Chi. When they did this, they felt nurtured and felt more whole, so they could then give more to others.

- 14% said they were not sure whether they consciously nurtured their psychological being, but when they felt stressed they wanted to take a vacation, go to a movie, go to a social function, or do something different like that.

- 14% said they felt healthy and good. Physically, they had always maintained good hygiene and personal care, which made them feel good psychologically as well.

- 14% said that their home business kept them in check, as they had to take care of their own issues as they arose, so that they were clear enough to support the people that came to see them for business; otherwise, they would not be able to serve others.

- 14% said they liked crossword puzzles, the arts, entertainment programs and the history channel on television. They loved learning and reading books that were non-fiction.

- 15% said they did many things through humor. This has served them well for many years. They also focused on being easy-going, while their spouses were more methodical. They did things for humor and from common sense, which was how they managed throughout life.

**Graph 3.9 Describe how you create your life to nuture your psychological being through feelings & how you feel about yourself? (Considering Retirement)**

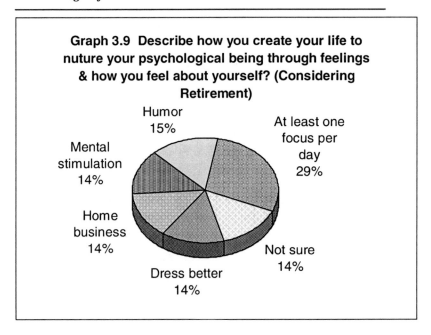

Humor 15%

At least one focus per day 29%

Mental stimulation 14%

Home business 14%

Not sure 14%

Dress better 14%

<u>Question:</u>  Describe how you create your life to nurture your spiritual being through personal values, spiritual values and standards of conduct.

Responses from Participants Considering Retirement were varied.  This is depicted below in Graph 3.10

- 43% believed in being honest and compassionate, believed in integrity, balance and harmony.  Harmony to them was like being in a flow, like the coming and going of the waves, the communion of harmony, the ying and yang, this type of thing. It was more harmony rather than balances, and is connected without knowing where one part starts and the other part ends. Retirement allowed for more flow. These participants said integrity, professionalism, confidentiality and ethics around their work was essential.

- 14% said they did not have spiritual values as most of their life was consumed with their work.

- 14% said they had a very strong ethical family. They were not church people, as they believed in the church of the great outdoors and nature, as everything came out of nature, and good surroundings.

- 29% said their work with their ministry, church, parenting through daily prayer and meditation was essential. They surrounded themselves with like-minded people for stimulating discussions knowing they were coming from the same perspective.

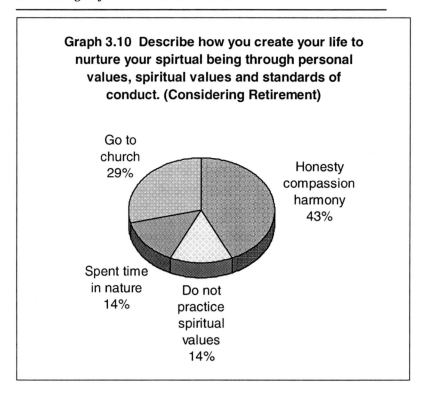

Graph 3.10 Describe how you create your life to nurture your spirtual being through personal values, spiritual values and standards of conduct. (Considering Retirement)

Go to church 29%

Honesty compassion harmony 43%

Spent time in nature 14%

Do not practice spiritual values 14%

**Question:** **Describe how you create your life to nurture your physical being through physical health, exercise and physical appearance.**

Responses from retired participants were as follows. This is depicted below in Graph 3.11

- All 100% of participants reported walking, gardening and physical work inside and outside their home.

- In addition to the above activities, 57% of participants retired for less than five years reported additional activities such as skiing, golfing, hiking, circuit training and swimming.

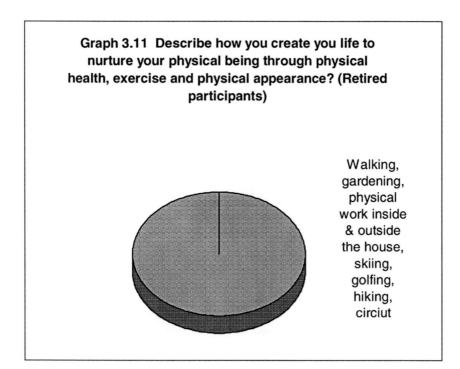

**Graph 3.11 Describe how you create you life to nurture your physical being through physical health, exercise and physical appearance? (Retired participants)**

Walking, gardening, physical work inside & outside the house, skiing, golfing, hiking, circiut

**Question: Describe how you create your life to nurture your psychological being through feelings and how you feel about yourself.**

Responses from retired participants were as follows. This is depicted below in Graph 3.12

• 10% reported walking.

• 10% reported writing letters.

- 10% reported watching television and reading.

- 10% reported working on crossword puzzles.

- 10% reported gardening.

- 10% reported taking nutritional supplementation.

- 10% reported humor.

- 10% reported meditation

- 20% reported sincerely helping and connecting with others with an open mind.

**Graph 3.12 Describe how you create your life to nuture your psychological being through feelings & how you feel about yourself? (Retired participants)**

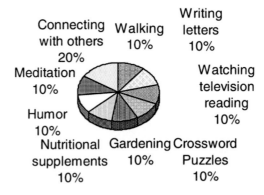

**Question:** Describe how you create your life to nurture your spiritual being through personal values, spiritual values and standards of conduct.

Responses from retired participants were as follows. This is depicted below in Graph 3.13

- 30% said they went to church.

- 10% said they did not go to church.

- 15% said they spend time in nature.

- 45% said they had good moral values, consciousness and respect for humans.

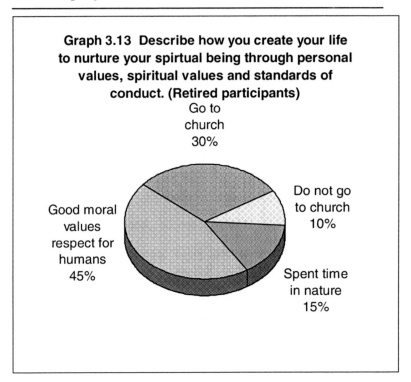

Graph 3.13 Describe how you create your life to nurture your spirtual being through personal values, spiritual values and standards of conduct. (Retired participants)

Go to church 30%

Do not go to church 10%

Good moral values respect for humans 45%

Spent time in nature 15%

**Question:** During your transition to retirement, how will you create psychological safety to reduce anxiety and create motivation?

Responses from participants considering retirement were as follows. This is depicted below in Graph 3.14

- 50% reported they reduce stress by connecting with friends, laughing, sharing personal stories, having fun, keeping busy at home, focusing on home life and family members.

- 20% of participants had made deliberate decisions to change their jobs within their organization to a less stressful job. This was like a weaning down period for them. It gave them an opportunity to become accustomed to being more at home, although they found they missed the action of their work place and interaction with their working peers. All of these participants felt it was helpful to consider having some goals.

- 10% said they did not experience any anxiety and had never been a person that was frustrated or worried about things. They felt their transition was probably different because they had a couple of years of paid non-work from their buy-out package prior to considering retirement.

- 20% said they really did not know and they would wait and see. They would talk to retired people to learn from their situation and then apply their learning into their own personal situation.

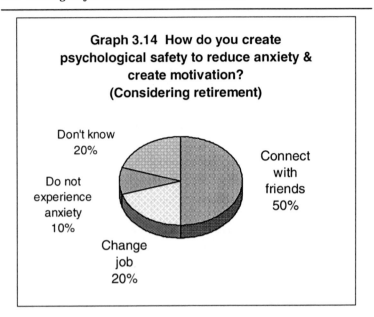

**Graph 3.14 How do you create psychological safety to reduce anxiety & create motivation? (Considering retirement)**

Don't know 20%

Do not experience anxiety 10%

Change job 20%

Connect with friends 50%

**Question:** **In your retirement, how do you create psychological safety to reduce anxiety and create motivation?**

Responses from retired participants were varied. This is depicted below in Graph 3.15

- 10% said they did not have any anxieties.

- 20% were active in body and mind through walking and reading.

- 10% said they took medication.

- 5% said they kept active in social justice issues.

- 15% said they went for acupuncture treatments.

- 10% said they spent time with their animals.

- 5% said they drank alcohol.

- 10% said they talked to themselves.

- 10% said they used self-hypnosis, meditation or deep breathing techniques.

- 5% said they spent time in their workshop using power tools.

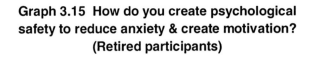

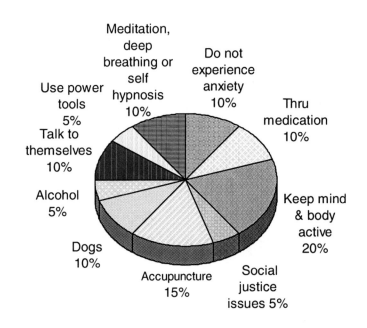

**Graph 3.15 How do you create psychological safety to reduce anxiety & create motivation? (Retired participants)**

Meditation, deep breathing or self hypnosis 10%

Do not experience anxiety 10%

Use power tools 5%

Thru medication 10%

Talk to themselves 10%

Alcohol 5%

Keep mind & body active 20%

Dogs 10%

Accupuncture 15%

Social justice issues 5%

## Question: How do you view retirement?

Responses from participants considering retirement were varied.

- 25% viewed retirement as both exciting and scary and they wondered if they would be bored and what they would do. They enjoyed working and knew they would miss their peers and the routine of going to work. They knew they needed to be with people.

- 25% looked forward to the change. They liked the idea of setting their own schedule. They knew the realities of aging were slowing them down physically and mentally and found it harder to keep up with the work pace.

- 25% said their work life had been very busy and stressful so they were looking forward to a break, doing something different on their own terms.

- 25% said they were looking forward to connecting with older people from all walks of life. They learned a lot from people they met over the years, and in aging, felt they could dress and say what they pleased because they were not subjected to the same peer pressures as they were in their workplace, or, as compared to being a teenager. There was a lot to celebrate about aging and about retirement.

## Question: How do you view retirement?

Responses from all retired participants were as follows.

- 25% reported that retirement was good for people, both physically and mentally. It was great to be paid by a pension and not go to work. Retirement was the prize for working all those years.

- 25 % reported that retirement was good if they could somehow work full time, then go to part time, then to less time, and eventually to no work at all. This they felt would give proper closure and they could then wean their way into something else.

- 5% reported that there should not be forced retirement at a specific age. If people enjoyed their job and were able to continue to do it well, they should keep working, if they wanted to, regardless of their age. If this was what people wanted, and it made them happy, they should continue. The unfortunate problem was that this might not allow the younger people an opportunity for employment.

- 20% reported they did not like retirement. They missed their peers, their paycheck, their work routine and their daily purpose. When they worked they felt valued in society and now retired, they did not feel like they were valued or contributing to society.

- 20% of participants reported that retirement was great, but the problem was that our culture does not value people if they are not making money. Some people had their identities tied up too strongly in their jobs, and when they retired, they felt lost. They had been so busy working all those years that they had forgotten about themselves and their being, spending their lives an a human doing as opposed to a human being.

- A value of 5% of participants reported that retirement was good if one had hobbies. It was important to keep busy.

**Question:** **How do you view your retirement goals?**

Responses from participants considering retirement were as follows.

- 71% said they had not set goals and they would just go with the flow and do whatever they felt like. They knew they wanted to spend some time with family, recreational activities and traveling but they were not really sure what else they wanted to do yet.

- 29% said they viewed their retirement goals positively as they believed in setting goals and working towards them, although they felt it was also important to be flexible knowing that their goals would not run their life.

## Question: How do you view your retirement goals?

Responses from retired participants were as follows.

- 75% of participants had not set retirement goals. They tended to drift where the wind blew them. Goals sounded too structured and concrete.

- 25% of participants had consciously set retirement goals such as traveling, maintaining physical health, mental health and spiritual well being.

**Question:** On a scale from one to five, one being low or poor and five being high or excellent, how would you rate your personal achievement of balance in your life? This is depicted below in Graph 3.16

- Considering retirement: average response at 3.8
- Retired less than five years: average response at 3.4
- Retired over five years: average response at 4.2

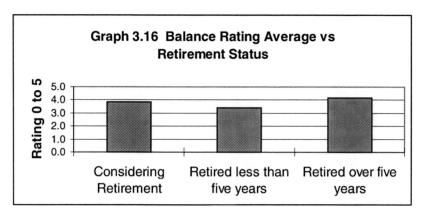

**Graph 3.16 Balance Rating Average vs Retirement Status**

## FINDINGS ON THE STAGES OF AGING IN RETIREMENT BY THE PARTICIPANTS

### Question: What is old age?

Perceptions of age changed as people aged. Responses from participants considering retirement were as follows.

- 43% of participants said that old age in our western cultural society sounded like we were falling apart, but in the eastern culture, old age made one wise. They summarized that old age meant the deterioration of the body.

- 47% said that old age was a mental state of mind that occurred when someone thought they were old. They felt there was a stage when the body was physically worn out and was old. If people thought they were old and finished, then this was true and they were. If people wanted to continue to live, they could, unless they were physically old, they were not mentally old.

- A sum of 10% of participants said there was no definition of old age because nobody ever got old. If one was talking about time as old age then, it could be 140 years.

## Question: What is old age?

Responses from all retired participants were as follows.

- 53% said old age was a physical and mental stage where the body and mind were starting to slow down and wear out. It was when people no longer had an open mind.

- 5% said old age was an illness.

- 25% said old age was when people were inactive physically and mentally, similar to people in old age homes.

- 10% said it was just another season or stage in their life.

- 7% said 65 years of age.

## Question: What is important to you as you approach old age?

Responses from participants considering retirement were as follows. This is depicted below in Graph 3.17

- All of participants said health was the most important aspect approaching old age. It was the same idea as taking care of their automobile as it aged. They were looking after their automobile and it was holding together. Their car had a few rough spots but they always looked after it and it was doing quite well, probably a lot better than some of the cars that were only four or five years old. So, they rationalized that by looking after themselves they might have a longer life than maybe someone younger that was on drugs or smoked. In health, mental health was most important. Even though the body slowed down, people hoped that their health was maintained.

- 5% said they could not answer this question because they did not consider themselves approaching old age. The important things in life were the same things that were important to them all along.

- 80% said that physical health was a big component and they hoped to keep their minds as they enjoyed educational programs, reading and good conversations.

- 15% said they did not think old age had anything to do with chronological age. It had everything to do with a person's state of mind. If people used their minds, they would keep their minds into old age. If people did not use their minds, they would lose their minds in old age therefore it was important to keep an active mind reading doing crossword puzzles for example.

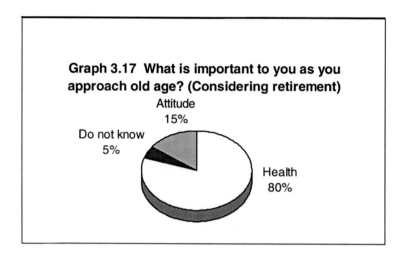

**Graph 3.17 What is important to you as you approach old age? (Considering retirement)**

Attitude 15%

Do not know 5%

Health 80%

## Question: What is important to you as you approach old age?

Responses from retired participants were as follows. This is depicted below in Graph 3.18

- 40% said spouse, family and friends.

- 10% said money.

- 40% said maintaining their health, both mental and physical capabilities for as long as possible.

- 5% said to stay active and independent.

- 5% said to feel that they were contributing value to society.

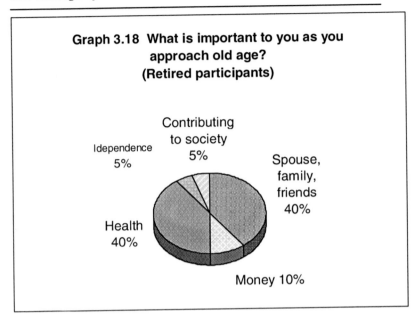

**Graph 3.18  What is important to you as you approach old age? (Retired participants)**

Contributing to society 5%

Idependence 5%

Spouse, family, friends 40%

Health 40%

Money 10%

**Question:** **What are your expectations for changes in health and longevity?**

Responses from participants considering retirement were as follows.

- 43% of participants said they tried very hard not to even think about expectations. They had a feeling they would live a long life but also believed that no one ever knew how life was going to treat them, therefore, they felt it was best to stay open to the whole idea of health and living a long life because sometimes we do not know how the cards will be dealt. They expected that some things may go wrong and some things would slide or just slow down.

They knew they did not have the strength of a teenager but hoped to maintain their health and activity levels.

- 28% said that longevity was on their side as all of their relatives had been healthy and there had not been cancer or anything like that in their family health history. They knew that eventually some of their body parts would wear out and that would be the end. They believed they could experience a long and healthy life provided they maintained their physical activities.

- 29% said longevity was not in their hands although they were not going to worry about it. They felt they were lucky as they had never really taken good care of their bodies, and yet, their bodies had done a very good job for them.

**Question:** **What are your expectations for changes in health and longevity?**

Responses from retired participants were as follows.

- 27% said their parents lived long so longevity was on their side.

- 20% said their parents did not live long so longevity was not on their side.

- 23% said they had to watch their eating habits and take nutritional supplements.

- 20% said they were not going to worry about it, and would just take one day at a time, and enjoy each day as it came.

- 5% said they did not want to end up decrepit in an old age home, and if they became a heavy burden on their families and suffered, they wanted to take control on their own terms and decide when and how they would leave the earth.

- 5% said they would need to maintain their exercise in order to maintain their longevity.

**Question: Describe the problems associated with living on a fixed income.**

Responses from participants considering retirement were as follows.

- 40% said that a fixed income was a concern to them and they would deal with that problem when the time came. They felt there would obviously be inflation, and they would probably lose their standard of living.

- 30% said they had lived on a fixed income all of their lives. This, they called a salary, so this was not something new. A pension was a fixed income.

- 20% said their buying power would be decreased over time, although, as their children aged, there would suddenly be a reduced spending requirement and more money would become available. There was not much point in having money if people could not spend it. They felt that people's fear in the future was that inflation would come back, and their buying power would disappear.

- 10% said they would have the same cheque book as they did now and they never had to live on a budget before. If they bought anything big, they talked to their spouse's about the purchase. The financial part of retirement, and the fixed income of a pension, was not going to produce a worry for them.

**Question:** **Describe the problems associated with living on a fixed income.**

Responses from all retired participants were as follows.

- 40% of participants were not too worried about living on a fixed income, as their company pension plan was indexed for inflation, and their RRSP's and other investments would top up their financial requirements nicely.
- 20% of participants were very concerned about inflation and health care costs into the future.
- 40% of participants said they would just have to budget and watch their spending just as they had always.

**Question:** **On a scale from one to five, one being low or poor and five being high or excellent, how would you rate your level of independence?**

This is depicted below in Graph 3.19

- Considering retirement: average response at 4.6

- Retired less than five years: average response at 3.9

- Retired over five years: average response at 4.4

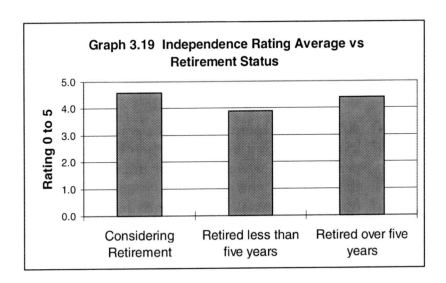

Graph 3.19 Independence Rating Average vs Retirement Status

## FINDINGS ON THE HISTORY OF RETIREMENT BY THE PARTICIPANTS

### Question:  What is retirement?

Responses from participants considering retirement were as follows.

- 14% said retirement was like taking a tire and re-tiring it, giving it more life, and a new life, or new treads.

- 29% said retirement was reaching the age of 60, and having a change in their work status.

- 14% said retirement was the change from actively producing goods or services to voluntarily producing goods or services.  They felt in retirement there was an element of choice and pleasure and less of a need to make money.

- 14% said retirement was enforced withdrawal from the workforce.  They believed this has contributed to a society that does not respect elders, and perhaps this had evolved itself into a self-fulfilling prophecy in that some elders no longer saw themselves as valuable because they were forced to walk away from the work force.  In our civilization, hundreds of years ago, it did not matter as people just worked and they were part of a community. Today people seem to have a strong identity attached to the type of work they do, and a large number of our western culture buys into that concept. So when people retire, they no longer have value and that is why there are a lot of miserable people in retirement. Education and planning was recommended but not always taken seriously by people. It seemed that people were out the door when they reached the age of 65 years. It did not matter if they were healthy, intelligent or if they were creating a most fantastic new concept. At 65 years of age it is *"bye, bye,"* which is pretty silly. These participants felt that retirement should be a choice, so people could make their own decision to deliberately pull themselves out of the mainstream work environment and become isolated, only by their choice.

- 29% said retirement was a changing of the workplace. Instead of coming to the workplace everyday, people stayed home and did other things. In both cases they enjoyed what they were doing. It was a change of lifestyle and an evolution, or a moving from one phase of working life into another phase of life. It was just a season in one's life.

## Question:  What is retirement?

Responses from all retired participants were as follows.

- 15% said it was learning to live on less money and less structure.

- 60% said it was the stoppage of work, no boss, no more working for someone or for yourself, no more making money from a work place.

- 10% said it was being 65 years of age.

- 15% of said it was receiving a pension and not having a requirement to work and a change in priorities.

## Question: Why are you now considering retirement?

Responses from participants considering retirement are as follows.

- 29% said health reasons.

- 14% said they were given a great buy out package to consider.

- 14% said age, as it was time for them to spend more time in their personal lives, their workshop, reading books they have not read, and taking time to do the things they wanted to do when they wanted to do them.

- 43% said financially they were now ready to take a look at retirement. They had worked long enough and it was now time to retire.

## Question: Why did you retire?

Responses from all retired participants are as follows. This is depicted below in Graph 3.20

- 30% said they were offered a good retirement package so they took it.

- 33% retired because of health reasons.

- 5% felt they were forced into retirement and wanted to go back.

- 17% said they had worked long enough and were now eligible to receive a good pension.

- 10% said the joy had gone out of their work and so they felt it was time to move onwards, to the next phase in their life.

- 5% said their spouse's were very ill and they did not know how much time they had together as a couple, so they retired to spend more time together.

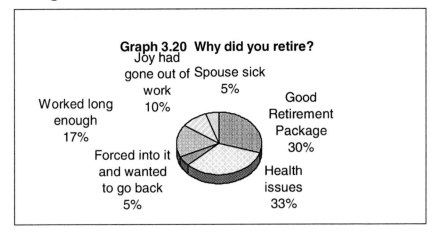

**Graph 3.20 Why did you retire?**

Joy had gone out of work 10%

Spouse sick 5%

Worked long enough 17%

Good Retirement Package 30%

Forced into it and wanted to go back 5%

Health issues 33%

## Question:  Do you think you will want to continue to work past the age of 65? Why or why not?

Responses from participants considering retirement were as follows.

- 14% said it depended on the number and times of working hours.  They did not want to work nine to five, but would consider a home-based business option.

- 24% said this was a few years into the future, and no one was good at predicting the future. They felt they could have some income generated from their hobbies, but they did not want to actively seek employment past the age of 60 years.  They felt it was good to retire young and enjoy good health, hobbies, friends and family.

- 5% said they were going to work on their home-based business as long as it suited them, which could be past the age of 65 years.

- 43% said financially they were able to retire early and were excited about it.

- 14% said they would not want to continue to work past the age of 65. They would probably get involved in some volunteer activities to keep busy.

**Question:** **Do you think you will want to continue to work past the age of 65? Why or why not?**

Responses from retired participants were as follows.

- 70% said absolutely no, not as the work place was today. They wanted to get on with life and enjoy time together with their spouse.

- 20% said they would not work on a full time basis, but they would consider a part time basis.

- 10% said yes, they loved their work.

**Question:** **What strategies would you recommend to people who are starting to plan for retirement?**

Responses from participants considering retirement were as follows.

- Attend a workshop on retirement and read books. They felt there was not enough available information out there yet for people to prepare themselves for retirement. People needed to look at different aspects of retirement and then slowly prepare themselves.

- Definitely, goal setting as people felt setting short and long goals are important for them to maintain some satisfaction, excitement and enjoyable challenges in their lives.

- Talk to people who are retired, have an open mind, apply and learn from stories of other people's experiences. People felt this type of activity would make them feel more comfortable with the concept of retirement before their time came along.

- Read books on transition. It was not the change; it was the transition that was the challenge in retirement. These periods of concern from the time people start thinking about retirement, until they are actually retired, up to the first two years of retirement. The big transition into their next phase of life. Retirement was just another phase. As people grew older, their health became more questionable, so people needed to consider the question - what to do if their health deteriorated?

- Get your financial life and family life in order.

- Everyone was going to have to choose a retirement strategy based on their own circumstance, and how they wanted to approach their retirement. The participants felt that people should think about the change and when they wanted to make the change. They felt the financial part of retirement was pretty obvious, but the psychological part involved more time for processing thoughts, planning, evaluating and then re-think the process after they had some time being in retirement. Some participants felt they needed the assistance of a counselor.

- Some participants felt there were very few opportunities in retirement to lessen the fear of change and so they wondered what do people actually do in retirement. These participants felt there was not much available information in layman's terms. There was an expressed need for a retirement transition program to address a variety of these aspects.

- Some participants were concerned about a couple of financial questions on whether to take the 100% pension and purchase insurance.

- Obtain a good financial advisor, attend retirement seminars and get some hobbies in place - whether it is exercise, woodworking, or exploring volunteer activities.

- Start an RRSP very early in life, do not wait until 40 years of age to start saving. Start saving and planning earlier on in life. Attend retirement seminars and learn about financial planning. Couples felt a need to start discussing their change and how they would manage change between themselves. Most people did not understand change so they did not plan for change.

**Question:** **What strategies would you recommend to people who are starting to plan for retirement?**

Responses from all retired participants were as follows.

- Pay off all debts including the house mortgage.

- Think long term about finances.

- Live on less than you earn and put away some money every month.

- See a financial advisor.

- Read books and attend retirement seminars.

- Think about the kind of expenses you would have in retirement and find out what your monthly expenses would be.

- Get involved in social activities, volunteer activities, community activities or hobbies before you retire, to keep yourself mentally happy, and to keep your spouse happy so that you are not at each other's throats.

- Maintain good relationships with family and friends

- Plan for physical, social and mental activities. Learn more about yourself for example, if you are ambitious, you need to find things to do, and keep busy so you do not get bored and depressed.

## <u>Question:</u>  How do you feel about retirement?

Responses from participants considering retirement were as follows.

- 20% said that after the interview they felt a lot better about retirement because they were starting to think about it. They were concerned about the financial aspect of retirement.

- 30% said they were looking forward to retirement.  They would be able to set the time to try and do the things they want to do.

- 25% said they were looking forward to it but at the same time were a little hesitant because they really enjoy working at their current jobs.

- 25% said they felt good about retirement. Time flies by and they felt that people did not start to think about retirement until it actually occurred, which was too late.  They felt that employers should provide education to inform employees to start thinking about retirement sooner.  Participants expressed a need to put a focus on retirement for people, to think about it earlier, plan, and learn from others.  By doing so, the participants felt people would not be in total shock when they entered retirement.

**<u>Question:</u>  How do you feel about retirement?**

Responses from all retired participants were as follows.

- 40% said retirement is wonderful if you have the material comforts and the right attitude.

- 40% said retirement is great and they have no hesitation in recommending it to anyone.

- 20% said it is all right except that they have too much time on their hands and they get lonely.

**<u>Question:</u>  What questions do you have regarding retirement?**

Responses from participants considering retirement were as follows.

- I don't have too many questions right now. I'm just wondering what it's going to be like. Will I travel?  Will I stay connected with people?  I know I'm going to miss the work place quite a bit. I need to focus on the transition so I can get used to the idea more slowly.

- Well, I don't know what I'm going to be up against.  I'm curious about what other people's experiences have been.  What other people may have gone through during their transition to retirement.  What factors did they have when it was a shock to them?  I know I will miss my peers and the type of work that I'm doing.

- I would like to hear of more opportunities for people that are retiring. Opportunities for life, such that it can provide a conduit.

- Well, it's sort of long term. Like, why are we doing that? Why does the workforce feel that it's necessary to oust people? Why is that at the last minute, there's gray hair. It is like you become invisible. Those kinds of things. Those types of questions. I think one's attitude is as important as anything to make your transition successful.

- Your questions are good in that they make you think. What are you going to do with your time when you've got all this time on your hands? And I've been thinking about it. And now I can delve deeper into this, perhaps. I know someone who just dreaded retirement because they didn't know what they were going to do with themselves. So if one doesn't have a hobby, then it is quite difficult. I know my mom was concerned about my dad when he retired. She found that he was difficult to handle. She wasn't used to having someone around the house. But eventually they came to an understanding and he got out of the house enough. He went golfing and they adapted, each in their own way. They've got their interests. They love traveling. They worried about retirement. They still had enough of their own lives to lead side-by-side without being in each other's way. And I hope that I'm developing enough interests outside of work so that it's not overtaking my world. So when I leave work I'm going to still have enough to keep myself busy.

**Question: On a scale from one to five, one being low or poor and five being high or excellent, how would you rate your attitude towards retirement?**

This is depicted below in Graph 3.21

- Considering retirement: average response at 4.5

- Retired less than five years: average response at 3.9

- Retired over five years: average response at 4.4

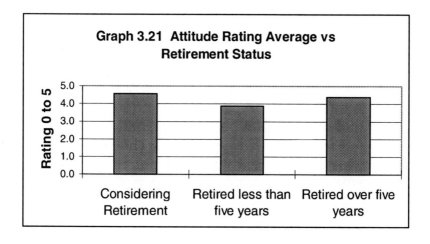

# CHAPTER FOUR – SUMMARY OF RESEARCH RESULTS

As a result of this research, the findings are delineated under three main groups, those considering retirement, those retired less than five years and those retired over five years. Under each group the researcher has identified six key areas of concern.

1. Health

2. Relationships

3. Know thyself

4. The paradox of time

5. Transitions en route to change

6. Finances

## PARTICIPANTS CONSIDERING RETIREMENT:

### 1. Health

A total of 43% of participants from this group had some type of health issue and generally felt they were slowing down. They felt they were not physically as strong as they were when they were younger, although 57% of these participants said they were in good health and were blessed with good genes. If they got an illness, their retirement would definitely be affected. At least 71% of these participants felt there was great value in maintaining their physical activities to support their health and stamina. They were concerned about taking care of themselves through physical exercise and nutritional supplementation for the prevention of disease. It was interesting to note that image was important to 29% of participants who dyed their hair and took hot baths. All participants agreed 100% that health was important to them as they approached old age. They were most concerned about keeping their minds in tact compared to any other illness. They felt old age was a mental state of mind as one was old only if they thought they were old, they could be physically old as the body wears out with age, but they did not have to be mentally old, so old age was a state of mind.

## 2. Relationships

A large number, 86% of these participants said family roles would not change too much in retirement. These participants would have more time for involvement with their family and friends. 43% of participants believed in being honest, compassionate and balanced. They believed that harmony was like being in the flow ...a connection without knowing where one part starts and the other part ends.

## 3. Know thyself

Considering these participants were still working they all agreed that once they retired they wanted to initially just relax and not do anything. After this initial rest period they wanted then to have more fun, travel, explore new hobbies or crafts. All of these participants agreed they needed to establish a routine in retirement because they enjoyed some structure in their life, although they also enjoyed their time for creativity. They felt they needed some types of boundaries to give them a sense of purpose so they would not lose focus and go all over the place. This was concern because they wondered how they would achieve this balance. Of these respondents, 50% agreed to find things to reduce stress during this transition such as keeping a connection with friends, laughing, sharing personal stories, having fun, focusing on home life, family and keeping busy at home. Looking at this need for structure it is interesting to note that 71% did not set goals, they wanted to go with the flow. It was important to spend time with family, rest, relax, travel and participate in recreational activities but they were not sure exactly what they wanted to do as they were still working and were just considering retirement. Participants wanted some time to reflect about retirement after they left the workplace and got off the work treadmill. Then they would have some time to reflect on what they wanted

to do in their retirement. They knew they
wanted element of flexibility, as their working
life had always been so busy and structured.
Just under half, 43% of these participants felt
they do not want to think about expectations
because who knows how long they will live or
what they will be confronted with in their life,
so they wanted to go with the flow and not
have expectations. They want to keep healthy
and active. They know they will live a long life.

## 4. The paradox of time

All of the participants agreed the most exciting
aspect of retirement seemed to be freedom of
time from scheduling, to do the things they
wanted to do when they wanted to do them
was a luxury concept. These participants
considering retirement could also see that they
would miss their working peers, and would
have to find a way to cope with that loss.

## 5. Transitions en route to change

To prepare for the change to retirement, 43%
of participants said they have attended
retirement seminars, read books and talked
with retired people. 14% of participants said
they did not really know how to prepare
themselves for retirement. They felt they
would just assume things and work towards
retirement and handle things on a daily basis.
15% of these participants did things through

humor and maintained an easy-going, coping mechanism. In the process of considering retirement, it was interesting to note that 20% of participants made deliberate decisions to change jobs to a less stressful position. This was like a weaning down period to reduce job stress but in doing so, they found they missed the action of the work place and their old job. One fifth or 20% did not know how to create psychological safety en route to retirement and felt they would wait and see and 25% viewed retirement as exciting and scary and looked forward to the change because they were getting tired of working and felt their health diminishing. They were looking forward to a change, to reduce stress from the busy life of full time work.

## 6. Finances

29% were concerned about money, while 57% of participants were not concerned about money. 40% of the participants felt that a fixed income would be a concern; on the other hand they had always lived on a fixed income throughout their life. There would not be much of a difference in retirement. They would still need to know how to budget and be responsible for their money. The great concern expressed by all was that of inflation and how it could impact their retirement savings and pension. The fear of future inflation was real. Would the retirement savings, company pension plan and investments provide sufficient dollars to maintain their current level of quality of life and comfort? No one wanted to reduce the quality of living style. They wanted to feel comfortable that it would be maintained. After all those years of working and saving, 43% felt they had worked long enough and it was now time to consider retirement; they had enough money saved from their company pension and investments and wanted to feel a sense of security that inflation would not take it all away from them. With these concerns, 20% of participants felt their buying power would be decreased over time and inflation would return.

## PARTICIPANTS RETIRED LESS THAN FIVE YEARS:

### 1. Health

A total of 60% of participants retired for less than five years said their health stayed the same as when they worked, while 25% said their health had actually improved as they had time to take better care of themselves, exercise and rest when they felt they needed to. 57% of participants said they enjoyed their physical activities such as walking, gardening, and skiing, golfing, hiking, circuit training, swimming and working inside and outside their home.

### 2. Relationships

At least 50% of participants said retirement had negatively affected their relationships as they had either moved away from where they worked, or some of their friends had moved away, or their friends were busy working, or their friends were working on shift work. As a result people felt lonely because they did not see their friends.

### 3. Know Thyself

25% of participants said retirement was good if they could have time to taper down from full time work to assist them to adapt into something else. A few, 5% said there should not be forced retirement at a specific age. They felt if a person enjoyed working they should be able to keep working regardless of age. On the other hand, they realized it was necessary to provide employment opportunities for the younger people. Some 20% of participants did not like retirement. They missed their working peers, paychecks, work routine and daily purpose. When they worked they felt valued in society and in their retirement they did not feel valued.

## 4. The paradox of time

A total of 75% of participants had no set retirement goals, they drifted where the wind took them; while 25% had retirement goals of travel, maintaining physical health, mental health and spiritual well bring. Old age was defined by 53% of the participants as a physical and mental state where the body and mind slowed down, 5% said it was an illness, 25% said it was when people were inactive, like people in old age homes and 7% defined it as 65 years of age. Retirement was defined by 15% as living on less money, 60% said it was the stoppage of work, having no boss, no more work or making money from a work place. One tenth of participants said it was being 65 years of age and 15% said it was receiving a pension and not having to work.

## 5. Transitions en route to change

30% retired because they were given a good
retirement package, although 5% said they
were forced into retirement and wanted to go
back, 17% said they had worked long enough
and were eligible for a good pension, 10% said
the joy had gone out of their work and it was
time to move on and 5% said they had a spouse
that was sick at home so they stopped working
to spent time together. An interesting statistic
was that 70% of participants said they would
not continue working, given the work place of
today, 20% said they would not work on a full
time basis, 10% said they would continue to
work. A 40% majority of participants felt good
about retirement if one had the material
comforts and the right attitude and 40% said
that retirement was great, while 20% said they
had too much time on their hands as they got
lonely and did not feel valued in society.

## 6. Finances

Many of the participants, 71% said they
started to think about retirement 5 to 15 years
prior to retirement. They had been saving
money in their registered retirement savings
plan, the company pension, then adding
additional money when it became available,
while 29% said they did not start to think
about retirement until a couple of months
before retirement. Also, 40% said they were
not worried about money as they had a good

pension and good investments, although 20% said they were concerned about inflation and health care costs in the future and 40% said they would just have to budget as they always had.

## PARTICIPANTS RETIRED OVER FIVE YEARS:

Participants retired over five years had similar comments to participants retired less than five years except for health, which is noted below. Results from both of these groups are discussed below in common themes between retired participants.

### 1. Health

15% said their health had deteoriated, although all 100% of participants did some type of physical activity such as walking, gardening and physical work inside or outside their home.

One very interesting observation from this group was that they had more definite answers to all of the questions posed in the interview. The had been retired over five years and had worked through their transition from working full time to their life in retirement. These participants nurtured their physical being through mild exercises. They nurtured their spiritual being by going to church, spending time in nature and practiced good moral values, consciousness and respect for humans. These participants created psychological safety to reduce anxiety and create motivation by 10% no anxieties, 20% keep active mind and body through walking and reading, 5% social justice issues, 15% acupuncture treatments,

10% spend time with animals, 5% alcohol, 10% talk to themselves, 10% self-hypnosis, 5% power tools. 25% said retirement is good for you physically and mentally, it is great to be paid by a pension, retirement is the prize for working all of those years, 20% said retirement is great but our culture does not value retired people if they are not making money, some people have their identities wrapped up too much in their work, they are out of balance, so when they retire they are lost, they have been busy working all of these years they do not know who they areas they are so wrapped up in their work, 5% said retirement is good if you have hobbies, it is important to keep busy.

## COMMON THEMES BETWEEN RETRED PARTICIPANTS:

### 1. Health

Both groups said 40% maintain health physical and mental capabilities for as long as possible was most important to them, while 40% said spouse, family and friends was most important to them, and 10% said money, 5% said to stay active and independent and 5% said contributing to society and doing things of value. Expectations for longevity - 27% said they had longevity on their side, 20% said they did not have longevity on their side, 23% said they had to watch their eating habits and take nutritional supplements, 20% said they were not going to worry about it and take one day at a time, 5% said they did not want to end up decrepit in an old age home and if they became a burden on their family they wanted to take control over their lives and decide when and how to leave the earth, 5% said they would have to maintain exercise to maintain their longevity. 33% said they retired because of health reasons.

### 2. Relationships

50% of participants said retirement had positively affected their relationships as they had more time to visit with family and friends, having more time to nurture relationships.

## 3. Know thyself

It is interesting to note that 50% of the participants said that they missed their peers, pay and structure of the work environment. They felt that time dragged on for them. Is seemed that there is considerable structure in the work environment and for less structure in retirement.

## 4. The paradox of time

50% of participants retired less than five years said they missed their working peers, their paycheck and the structure of work. 50% said there was nothing they disliked about retirement and 100% of all participants agreed that they enjoyed having this new freedom to do the things they wanted to do when they wanted to do them.

## 5. Transitions en route to change

53% of participants said old age was a physical and mental state where the body and mind slowed down, while 10% said old age was just another season in one's life.

## 6. Finances

71% of participants said they started to think about retirement 5 to 15 years before retirement. Over the years they had saved money in their registered retirement savings plan and company pension, while 29% said they did not start to think about retirement until a couple of months before retirement.

## COMPARISON OF GROUP FINDINGS:

The researcher has identified six themes summarized from the findings. These themes are health, relationships, know thyself, the paradox of time, transitions en route to the change and finances.

One participant stated that retirement is like "taking a tire and re-tiring it and giving it more life, a new life or new treads."

But they did not like the idea of retirement as "being in a state of rest." They believed it is better viewed as another season of life.

The majority agrees, except for the financial part that retirement is something to look forward to. The majority of the participants said:

> It is almost like opening up a Christmas present because you do not know what is inside. Retirement is reaching the age of 60 years and having a change in work status, or a change from actively producing goods or services to voluntarily producing them because of choice or pleasure.

On the other side, participants perceived retirement as:

...An enforced withdrawal from the workforce, which has contributed to a society that does not respect elders, and perhaps elders are self-fulfilling this prophecy as they no longer see themselves as valuable because they are forced to walk out of the work force. In our civilization, hundreds of years ago, this did not matter, as people worked and were viewed as part of a community. Today, many people attach a strong identity to the type of work they do, and a large percentage of our western culture population buys into that concept. So, when some people retire they feel they no longer have value, and that is probably why there are a lot of miserable people in retirement. It is like you turn 65 years of age and you are out the door. It does not matter if you are healthy, intelligent, or if you are creating the most fantastic new concept. At 65 years of age it is bye bye, which is pretty silly. Retirement should be a choice where people decide themselves if they want to deliberately pull themselves out of the mainstream work force and become isolated.

Another perceived notion is that retirement is the change of one's workplace.

Instead of coming to the workplace everyday, you stay home and do other

things. You enjoy what you are doing.
Retirement is a change of lifestyle and a
movement from one phase of working life
into another phase of retirement life. It is
just a season in one's life.

Is was interesting to note that 50% of the retired
participants said retirement had positively
affected their relationships with family and
friends as they experienced more time freedom to
visit with family and friends. All participants
agreed they had more time for themselves, others,
social contacts and social activities. There is no
rush to get to work and less structure during their
day. The following graphs represent responses
from those considering retirement and those
retired.

In this study 43% of participants considering
retirement and 33% of retired participants
considered retirement due to personal health
issues. It was felt that in aging, the body slows
down and most participants did not feel physically
as strong as they did when they were younger.
They did notice their metabolism slowing down.
57% of participants considering retirement felt
they had average to good health now, while 43%
had experienced a major deterioration in their
health, however 60% of retired participants had
average to good health while 15% had experienced
major deterioration in their health. Out of this

group, 25% experienced improved health up to the first five years in retirement.

For example, some participants said their legs felt better as they no longer had to wear work boots, or their chest and breathing had cleared up as they no longer worked with chemicals, or their back was less painful as they no longer had to walk or stand as much. They seemed to have a bigger smile on their faces.

For those participants who retired because of health issues, there was more time for them to reflect and rest. More time to stop, plant the roses, smell the roses and pick the roses. It was a time for them, to experience freedom from schedules and to do the things they wanted to do when they wanted to do them.

Marshall (1993) suggests that as aging progresses, people become more aware that their own time on earth is limited. Marshall (1980) suggests that the vast majority of older people come to terms with their mortality, but that such concerns do not become salient for most people until some time in their seventies. At that time they experience more of their peers dying, and they become concerned that their own death be appropriate. Most people do not want to live forever. They want to die feeling that they had a meaningful and dignified life. That is why the ability to remain independent, both physically and economically, and the ability to maintain family and affectionate bonds, is so critically important to the aged. The following graphs represent responses from those considering retirement and those retired.

A total of 14% of participants considering retirement were presented with a good-buy out package from their employer. This provided them an incentive to seriously consider retirement. A value of 30% of the retired participants were presented with a good retirement package which assisted them in their decision making process. Both groups felt that after working for many years, they had contributed sufficiently to RRSP's, their company pension plan, and others plans, and were ready to consider retirement.

Within the retired participants group, 71% started planning financially for retirement five to fifteen years prior to retirement, while 29% took the last minute approach. Some participants said that a fixed income was a concern to them but they would deal with that when the time came. They felt there would be inflation and their standard of living would be diminished. For those who had children, they felt their buying power would decrease over time as their children aged, resulting in a reduced requirement for spending, so more money would become available for themselves. Some participants said they have lived on a fixed income all of their lives, called a salary, and this was not something new. For example their pension would be their fixed income or salary in retirement and they would have to learn how to live on it.

Kelloway (1994) suggests some people will believe they have handled their retirement planning if they have a company pension and Canada Pension Plan as someone else is taking care of things for them, while other people will get actively involved in their own retirement by planning through RRSPs, insuring they have an income and not relying on those external supports so much. The same thoughts apply for planning quality in their lives. People who plan their lives will probably have a more satisfactory retirement because they are motivated and in control of their own destiny. The following graphs represent responses from those considering retirement and those retired.

In preparation for retirement 14% of retired participants said they had retirement goals, 14% said they had no retirement goals, 43% prepared themselves for retirement by reading books and attending retirement seminars and 29% focused their retirement preparation in the area of financial planning. Of the participants considering retirement, 71% said they had not set goals and they would just go with the flow and do whatever they felt like. They knew they wanted to spend some time with family, traveling and participating in recreational activities, although they were not really sure what they wanted to do as yet. The remaining group, which was 29% of participants considering retirement said they viewed their retirement goals positively and they believed in setting goals and working towards them, although they felt it was also important to be flexible knowing that their goals would not run their life. After speaking with the retired participants, it appeared that it was important to set goals. In regards to this, one participant said:

> ...That is what is done at work and that is how people get through work. Whether goals are set consciously or whether other people set them, this is important. In retirement, if I want to be active and focused on health rather than illness, I have to be organized; I have to have those things that keep me stimulated, which are goals. Now when I say that I am going to have to do what I want, when I want, that will be within my structure, although a very loose structure. I think people are most healthy emotionally, spiritually and physically, when they are valued, contributing and leading purposeful lives.

In the Canadian Press Newswire, Kelloway, (1994) a psychology professor at the University of Guelph. Suggests that planning for a successful retirement involves more than just financial goals and strategies. People are better off when they have a sense of purpose.

> Satisfaction in retirement is connected to the same factors involved in those found at work. That is, having a sense of purpose and contact with people outside the family...it wouldn't hurt at least in the initial period after retirement to have concrete plans as opposed to saying `well I can travel' or something vague and general. (p. 1)

> Kelloway (1994) further suggests: Retirement activities have to be challenging to be satisfying. Puttering around the garden or idly picking up a book is not going to be enough. The things that make people happy are goals and challenges that let them hone their skills or develop new ones. (p.72)

Psychologically, half of all participants said they had decided that when they reached a certain age they would retire. That age ranged from 55 to 60. Several participants started to think about retirement as they felt their health deteriorating. Others felt they deserved a break from the working environment once they reached their desired age of retirement and looked forward to more unstructured leisure time.

During their transition to retirement a few participants changed their jobs to less stressful positions to start a weaning process into retirement, although most did not consider the impact of psychological change of a busy, structured work life phasing into retirement life.

Of participants considering retirement, 57% said they would not work past the age of 65 years, 14% would not work from nine to five but consider a home-based business and 24% were not sure. Within the retired participants group, 70% said they would not work past the age of 65 years, 20% said they would not work full time but consider part time employment and 10% said they would definitely consider working past the age of 65 years.

At the beginning of retirement all participants considering retirement initially wanted to just relax and do nothing for up to one year, after that they wanted to have more fun, travel and discover hobbies or crafts. Several participants wanted to fix up their homes, do more reading, possibly some writing, volunteer activities, traveling and physical activities such as skiing, biking and sailing. Participants felt it was important to replace or repair large items in their home such as automobiles, appliances, roofs and painting while they had money, health and energy in the earlier years of retirement.

There are many people who view retirement as a paid vacation for the rest of their lives. Boulmetis (1997) suggests that:

> Somewhere between the sixth and fifteenth month of retirement they begin to wonder what else there is. (p. 15)

After the first few years into retirement it seemed that health was important to those participants who had retired. After taking care of themselves for the first few years of retirement, 25% of the participants said their health improved. Some participants said that taking care of their own health was like taking care of an automobile as it ages. Their automobile may have a few rough spots but generally it is doing quite well, probably a lot better than some of the automobiles that are only four or five years old. So by looking after themselves, they might have a longer life than maybe someone younger that is on drugs, or a smoker. Of the participants considering retirement, 80% said health was important to them as they approached old age, and 15% said that about keeping their minds sharp was important to them, while 5% were just uncertain what was important to them. Health is essential, even though the body may slow down. Participants still hoped that their health and mental capacities would be maintained well into their retirement years.

As the years went by the statistics changed slightly as 40% of retired participants said their health was important, 40% also said their spouse, family and friends were important to them as they approached old age, while 10% said money, 5% said independence and 5% said contributing to society were important.  People seemed to maintain their health as long as they could, but it seemed that as health deteriorated, it was replaced even more with the need for friendship, love and the human connection.  It was also interesting to note that financial concerns began to creep into the picture if finances were low.

All retired participants agreed that having freedom of time, to do the things they want to do when they want to do them such as hobbies, sports, crafts and spontaneous activities was a definite asset of retirement today and in the future.  Most retired couples enjoyed spending more time together and traveling.  For those participants who were not married, most appreciated their family, friends and animals that provided them with friendship, love and the human touch.  They liked the fact that they had lived a very full life and still looked forward to each and every day.  They had the time to reflect and look back to where they had been, and evaluated what they did and enjoyed living in the now.  Luxury items were really not all that important to them.  Some retired participants no longer drove their automobile, but were happy because they had a spouse.  They savored and appreciated living in the now, even though some days were not as nice as others. They still lived in the now and appreciated their time together. What was most important to them was knowing and having people close to their hearts and being together.

The study revealed that 14% of participants considering retirement had enough mental stress from the work place which made them initially consider retirement, while 10% of the retired participants felt they had no joy left in their work and 5% had a spouse who was sick at home so they chose to retire to be with their spouse. Also 5% felt they were forced out of the workplace and wanted to go back but felt they could not go back. Of participants considering retirement, 29% said they felt they had worked long enough and it was time to retire.

50% of responding participants considering retirement created psychological safety to reduce anxiety and create motivation by connecting with family and friends while 20% changed their jobs to a less stressful job, 10% said they did not experience anxiety and 20% just did not know. Furthermore, 25% of retired participants created psychological safety to reduce anxiety and create motivation by keeping an active mind and body, 15% had acupuncture treatments, 10% meditated or did deep breathing or self hypnosis, 10% talked to themselves, 10% did not experience anxiety,

10% took medication, 10% spent time with their dogs, 5% drank alcohol and 5% spent time in the workshop with power tools.

A total of 29% of those responding participants considering retirement nurtured their psychological being by having daily goals, 14% were not sure, 14% made a point of dressing themselves better, 14% focused on their home based business, 14% exercised their mind mentally through reading and doing crossword puzzles and 15% focused their efforts on humor, additionally 10% of the retired participants nurtured their psychological being by walking, 10% through writing letters, 10% by watching television, 10% through gardening, 10% by taking nutritional supplements, 10% through humor, 10% through meditation and 20% by sincerely helping and connecting with others.

A 71% majority of participants considering retirement nurtured their physical being through exercise such as walking, gardening, biking, golfing and skiing, while 29% dyed their hair and started to enjoy taking hot baths, cumulatively 100% of retired participants nurtured their physical being through physical exercise such as gardening, walking, hiking, golfing, skiing and working inside and outside the house.

A total of 43 % of participants considering retirement nurtured there spiritual being by being in harmony, being honest and compassionate. Of those responding, 14% said they did not practice spiritual values, 14% spent time in nature and 29% went to church. 30% of participants retired nurtured their spiritual needs by going to church, 10% did not go to church, 15% spent time in nature and 45% by having good moral values and respect for humans.

All participants said they needed to establish a routine because they enjoyed some structure in their life, although they also enjoyed time to be creative. They felt they needed to have some boundaries to give them a sense of purpose, otherwise they would lose focus and go all over the place, yet, and they did not want too much structure or routine.

Kelloway (1994) suggests, while employed, people devote most of their thoughts and energies to their career, not retirement.

> It's hard to imagine retirement...you can imagine a vacation, which is three weeks of not working, but now try to imagine 20 years and it's quite a different matter. (p. 2)

Kelloway (1994) suggests, it's not that you don't need structure any longer, you do, but it's one you can plan to suit your life. On one hand there are some people who think they are very much the masters of their own destiny...and there are others who think that everything that happens to them is luck or chance.

In our western culture, old age sounds like we are falling apart, but in the eastern culture, old age makes us wise. So is old age the deterioration of the body? Are we like old automobiles falling apart? Most participants said old age was a mental state of mind that occurred when someone thinks they are old. Traditionally there is a stage when the body is physically worn out and it is old. If one thinks they are old and finished then they are. If one wants to continue to live, one can. If one is physically old, they do not have to be mentally old. Attitude makes a world of difference in aging.

A few participants viewed retirement as both exciting and scary as they wondered if they would be bored and what they would do. They enjoyed working and knew they would miss their peers and the routine of going to work. They knew they needed to be with people and they were concerned about depression. They wondered if they would self sabotage them but knew that there was a lot to celebrate about aging.

A couple of participants retired less than five years were very concerned about the amount of taxes they were paying in retirement as well as inflation, and how their current financial status and retirement pension would maintain their lifestyle into the future. This was observed even though some participants had good retirement packages. Some participants said they would definitely have less money and routine and those retired found the longer they were retired, the harder it was to get into a structure or routine. Participants retired over five years realized they were growing older and had to face some of the frailties of life.

50% of retired participants missed their work peers, the mental stimulation of their work place, their paycheck and the structure of work. Participants alluded that represented a major change in their lives since leaving the work force. A value of 50% of the retired participants said retirement had negatively affected their relationships with family and friends as their friends were still working and sometimes on shift work so it was difficult to know when to call them. These participants felt that their time during the day tended to drag on a bit too long and those who moved away from where they worked missed their working peers, neighborhood and other social contacts.

# CHAPTER FIVE – RESEARCH CONCLUSIONS

The conclusions are delineated under the seven main themes that are: health, relationships, know thyself, the paradox of time, transitions en route to change, finances and seeing systems in retirement.

## 1. Health

- As people age, they unanimously agree that health is the most important factor in their life.

- The majority of people retire because of health concerns.

- People are concerned about health care facilities and health care options.

- In health, people are concerned firstly about keeping their mind in tact, and secondly about maintenance of their body.

- Over 70% of people say they would not return to the workplace after retirement based on how the workplace is today.

- Most individuals retired less than five years found their health was the same as when they were working, and 15% found that their health actually improved, as they felt they had more time to take better care of themselves. People retired over five years felt their health had deteriorated since the beginning of their retirement.

## 2. Relationships

- As people age, relationships are the second most important factor in their retirement life.

- The majority of people felt that family roles would not change too much in retirement.

- In spousal relationships, territorial boundaries were a concern.  For example, if the wife was already retired or at home and then the husband came home, the kitchen felt congested. The wife was accustomed to having her *"space"* and now that the husband was home she felt that her *"space"* was invaded or disappeared.

- Half of the people felt that retirement had negatively affected their relationships with family and friends.  People felt lonely if anyone moved away, or if their friends were still working.

- Half of the people felt that retirement had positively affected their relationships because there was more time to enhance relationships with family and friends.

## 3. Know thyself

- As people aged, knowing themselves was the third most important factor in their retirement life.

- People considering retirement want to spend the first year of retirement relaxing. After many years of working they want to be free from schedules, meetings and free to use their time as they please. This first year is a time of reflection and planning for the next phase in life. During this time they may also consider home repairs, new hobbies, crafts or travel. Upon further investigation, some people do not partake in certain activities because of the associated costs.

- People need boundaries and a sense of purpose to bring meaning to their life, therefore in retirement it is important to establish a routine. People enjoy some structure, as they are accustomed to having structure for many years in their structured working life.

- The transition to retirement is good for people if they had a period to wean down from a busy working schedule. While still working, some people made a conscious choice to move to a less stressful job. This move assisted them in their transition. Other people felt like they just flew off the treadmill when they finished working, and so they were in a state of distress because they missed the habitual treadmill. They were so accustomed to their busy working life that once they retired it took them awhile to wind down.

- Half of the people find they need to look at ways of reducing stress during their transition. They are not really sure what they want to do in retirement. Half of the people miss their working peers, paycheck and the structure of the work environment. Many people retired over five years seemed more at peace and confident as they had time to reflect on their working life, then moved into their life in retirement.

- It is a sad conclusion that our culture does not value retired people if they are not making money.

- If people are too wrapped up in their work such that when they retire they are lost, they do not know who they are, they are out of balance; it takes them approximately three to five years to regain their personal balance, to find out who they are, what is important to them, and start to live their life path.

- It is important to learn what we feel is valuable in life, and use our time valuably.

- Time must be valued as it is not an indispensable commodity. The way it is valued provides meaning to you.

- People in retirement have a right to live their passion and be valued. They may need to rediscover their passion in retirement life.

- Half of the people missed their working peers, work environment and paycheck.

- Retired people should not feel they have too much time on their hands. Consider an adult mentor for gifted children in schools.

- Our society has too many stigmas about retired people as noted in school Readers - little old lady stories. We have created myths and stigmas in children at an early age. If we expect to see a future with opportunities for retired people, we need to change how we view older persons.

- If we are going to make a difference, we need to start now.

## 4. The paradox of time

- As people age, the paradox of time is the fourth most important factor in their retirement life.

- The most exciting aspect of retirement is time freedom, freedom to do what you want, when you want, and those considering retirement see this as a luxury in life. The irony is that ten to fifteen months into retirement, people began to wonder, what else is there in life? They had too much time on their hands.

- People felt that as time went by, the body aged, but people felt they had choice to keep their mind young. People felt that if they exercised they could keep their body younger or in better shape as compared to those who did not exercise.

- An overwhelming 75% of people considering retirement, or newly retired had no retirement goals. Some people felt that goals were too structured even though they missed structure in their life.

- A sad conclusion was that half of the people missed their work environment, their peers and paycheck. They mostly missed the feeling of creating value over time for society.

- Half of the people retired over five years were content in their retirement. Harmony was like being in the flow ... a connection without knowing limits of time, where one part starts and the other part ends.

## 5. Transitions en route to change

- As people age, transitions en route to change is the fifth most important factor in their retirement life.

- There is a need to cope for the loss of the work environment, peers and paycheck.

- Some people are not aware of ways of creating psychological safety in periods of transition, they have a wait and see attitude.

- People view retirement as exciting and scary. They want a change from years of working, just for the sake of change, to do something different in their life.

- To prepare for the change from retirement to working, read books on change, attend retirement seminars and talk to retired people.

- Don't just assume everything will work out, think about your life, reflect, plan, implement your plan and then think about your life, reflect, plan, implement your plan, etc....

- Do things through humor and maintain an easy-going attitude.

- Retirement is another season in life.

## 6. Finances

- As people age, finances are the sixth most important factor in their retirement life. There was no doubt that money was important in retirement life, but health and relationships had a higher priority, after all if you did not have your health and friends, how could you enjoy your money?

- People budget throughout their working lives, budgeting in retirement is not much different.

- The greatest fear was that inflation could come back and erode ones savings and retirement pension.

- No one wants to reduce the personal quality of living or comfort in retirement. They want to maintain a similar quality and lifestyle as when they were working.

- Financially most people start to think about retirement five to fifteen years prior to retirement.

- Most people contribute either to registered retirement savings plans, the company pension plan or other investments.

- Most people did not think of the psychological transitions to retirement, although all of the participants of this research project were most grateful of their opportunity to discuss, reflect and learn more about themselves through the interview and transcript review process.

• From the time people start to consider retirement, to the time they have been retired less than five years to over five years, people go through a personal evolution.

### 7. Seeing systems in retirement

Each group of participants underwent emotional tensions from the time they started to consider retirement, to the time they entered retirement, through to their living years in retirement life. Each phase is depicted in a systems diagram highlighting major times of transition. This information is helpful to all for strategies for transitions to retirement. These phases are:

- Yearning for time
- The Paradox of time
- Life is a continuum

By looking at the different phases of retirement life, we can learn from the participants' comments and compare their comments to the current body of knowledge. Now in the end, we unveil processes of change rather than snapshots or cause-effect problem-solving chains.

## Yearning for Time

People considering retirement all yearn for time freedom. They look forward to having more control over time in their life. They want to own their time and do the things they want to do when they want to do them. Figure 5.1 Yearning for Time, depicts the first phase in transitions to retirement. People considering retirement want more time freedom. People wanting time freedom consider retirement. In this phase people bounce back and forth before they make their decision for the best time to retire.

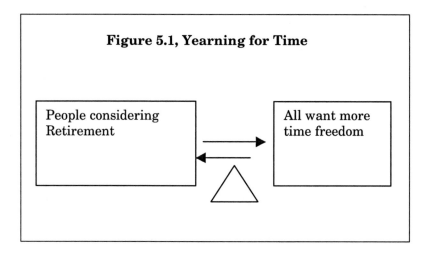

**Figure 5.1, Yearning for Time**

People considering Retirement

All want more time freedom

## The Paradox of Time

Once a person retires, they savor their time freedom by sleeping in, reading the newspaper in bed or by sipping on an extra cup of coffee as they leisurely wake up in the morning. In essence they are nurturing themselves, after all those years of working, they deserve an opportunity to gear down or to stop and smell the roses. Some people nurture their physical being through making time for exercising, while others nurture their homes and install a new roof, paint or change their landscaping. They are fine-tuning their abode by making it more maintenance free and comfortable for the years to come.

When people first retire, they are happy to have this time freedom, but after approximately ten to fifteen months, some people reach the gap of bewilderment. They find they miss their working peers, the structure of work life and their paycheck. They miss the feeling of contributing to society and the feeling of being valued. People begin to wonder what is the next task in their life, or deeper yet, what is important to them now in life. Life in retirement is different from working life. So, people take some time to think about this, they make some decisions and some people set some goals. This thinking cycle spirals and continues until the retired person reaches their desired state of feeling valued in society. To get to this point some people return to part-time work, start a home-based business or become involved in volunteer activities. As noted below in Figure 5.2, The Paradox of Time, the systems viewpoint is generally oriented toward the long-term view or desired state of feeling valued in society. That is why the delay and feedback loops are so important. In the short term, one can often ignore these loops as they are inconsequential, but they come back to haunt people in the long term if they have not resolved their personal issues.

**Figure 5.2, The Paradox of Time**

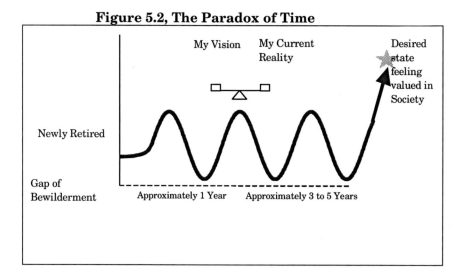

Now within the Paradox of Time, emotional tensions occur between people's reality and their vision. This is heightened ten to fifteen months into retirement. This happens then because people need the initial months of retirement to gear down from work life, carrying on with tasks they were too busy to do while they were working. After these initial months, people then begin to wonder what to do next?

People achieve extraordinary results with extraordinary visions, where their results happen to be different from their original intent. Making choices and looking closely at current reality can also bring deeply buried emotions to the forefront. These emotions could depress people initially, and then excite them later. Emotions are part of the transition process in retirement. These emotions are not necessarily good or bad, they just appear during these transition times. It is important to acknowledge emotions and learn how to work with them. This can be a balance act for some people, depending on their level of personal acceptance of themselves and their situation.

## Life is a continuum and retirement is part of that continuum:

Who is the retired person and what is important to them? These answers are essentially the same values important to people when they are working. Life is a continuum and retirement is part of that continuum, therefore it is important to value people regardless of their age or stage in life, as they are all part of the same process of life. People are now living longer and healthier than ever before. People's needs do change as they get older and their needs are met in different ways, so why are retired people put in glass bowls? For example, why do some people talk down to retired people? Why are some retired people alienated because of their age? Why are they valued in society up to the age of 65 years, and then asked to leave the workplace? These types of example set the tone for the value people place on retired people in society.

Figure 5.3, The Heart of the Matter shows the continuum of life. Instead of having the retired person feeling lost or out of place, they are embraced as they are just as productive/important as the working class of people. Encourage retired people and surround them with the aspects important to them, and they will feel valued and contribute to society.

Government and organizations need to recognize this current mind-set as the large baby-boomer population heads to retirement. What impact will this current mind-set have on the future? Knowing this, how can we consider changing the mindset on how people view retired people and get them out of the glass bowl? It is important that Government and organizations conduct research to address these concerns before the baby-boomer population retires. It is beneficial that Government provide incentive programs and intergenerational activities, as well as organizations to provide opportunities for retired people so that both the organization and the retired people benefit.

## Figure 5.3, The Heart of the Matter

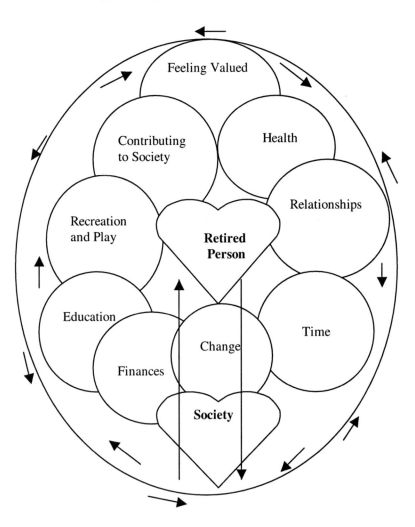

# CHAPTER SIX – RECOMMENDATIONS FOR FURTHER ACTION

Based on the findings and conclusions, the following recommendations are made. These recommendations are divided into three separate groups who can consider further research or initiation of these recommendations.

## Government

- Provide choices and incentives for retirement instead of forced retirement at 65 years of age.

- Encourage the development of programs relating to disease prevention through nutritional supplementation, diet and exercise for retired individuals.

- Determine amenable living arrangements in retirement communities, suited and adapted to meet the needs of the physical being, having health as the qualifier, not age, as we cannot afford to neglect those who are healthy and mentally sharp.

## Organizations

- Encourage the development of programs for health promotion with a focus on exercises for the mind and body.

- Provide seminars to employees on how to create passion and value in retirement life.

- Provide seminars to employees on psychological transitions to retirement and change in general.

- Develop retirement workshops that teach people how to use computers so they can keep in touch with their working peers and assist themselves in the prevention of loneliness in retirement.

### Individuals

- Have people consider weaning down to a less stressful job prior to retirement.

- Teach people to start thinking about their life in retirement today, their hobbies, activities and ways they would like to contribute value to society.

- Teach people to plan consistent investment strategies for retirement savings.

- Talk to retired people to hear their personal experiences and learn from them prior to retirement.

## PLANNING SUCCESSFUL STRATEGIES FOR TRANSITIONS TO RETIREMENT

Based on comments from all of the participant interviews, the following recommendations were made for planning successful strategies for transitions to retirement.

- You will need to plan a strategy based on your own circumstance and how you want to approach retirement, so think about the change and when to make the change.

- While you are still working get involved in some hobbies, whether they are sports, crafts, volunteer activities, family activities or other social functions. There is more to life than work, so try not to have your personal identity tightly bound up in your profession.

- If you feel you have a very stressful job, consider changing your job within your organization to a less stressful job, or work part time. This psychological downsizing of work stress will assist you to reduce anxiety in your psychological being and most likely enhance your personal self worth.

- Attend a retirement workshop and read books. There is not enough information out there yet for people to retire. People need to look at different aspects of retirement and slowly prepare themselves.

- Read books on transition. "I agree, it is not the change, it is the transition that is the challenge, from the time people start thinking about retirement until they are actually retired up to the first two years of retirement. As people grow older their health becomes more questionable so people need to consider that question - what to do if their health goes. This is a big transition into their next phase of life. It is just another phase.

- Definitely set some goals and start to think about retirement while you are working. What are you going to do five years from now? What are you going to do ten years from now? Writing these goals down can set your unconscious into action. This can be very exciting. This process can help you deal with your fears and help you think about your aspirations in retirement. On the flip side, if you have no written goals you will probably end up drifting like a cork on the sea, with no purpose. Is that where you see yourself in the future?

- Talk to people who have retired to feel more comfortable with it before your time comes along to retire.

- There are very few opportunities in retirement to lessen the fear of change, so get to know more about how you personally handle change. For example does change excite you or scare you. Get to know how you handle different circumstances. Do you recharge your batteries when you are alone or with people around you?

- Couples need to start talking about retirement between them. This is a part of change and managing change. Most people do not understand change so they do not plan for change.

- Talk to a financial planner and get your financial future in order.

- Start an RRSP early, while you are working and do not wait until you are 40 years old to start saving. Save a little money every month, no matter what the income. Learn about financial planning.

# CHAPTER SEVEN – RESEARCH IMPLICATIONS

## General Implications

The baby boomer generation has been the leading force of social, cultural and economic changes in Canada during the last four decades. Statistics indicate that by 2011, one in five Canadians will be over 65 years of age as compared to one in ten in the early 1990's. Canada, like many other countries, is experiencing a significant aging of its population. This trend is expected to lead to an increase in burdens on public sector funds for pensions, health care and seniors' programs. These burdens are dependent on demographic change, economic growth and structural aspects of the public sector age-sensitive programs. The baby boomers are heading towards retirement. Data indicate that Canadians are continuing to take a last-minute approach to retirement.

People need to start thinking about retirement while they are working. Taking a last minute approach may cause grief. Employers can add the aspect of psychological planning and transitions to retirement to their retirement planning repertoire. Some comments from research participants on psychological transitions to retirement are:

- "Everyone is going to have to choose a retirement strategy based on their own circumstance, and how they want to approach their retirement. People should think about the change and when they want to make the change."

- "Your questions are good in that they make you think. What are you going to do with your time when you've got all this time on your hands? And I've been thinking about it. And now I can delve deeper into this perhaps."

- "I need to focus on the transition so I can get used to the idea more slowly."

- "I think your attitude is as much as important as anything to make your transition successful."

- "Why does the workforce feel that it's necessary to oust people? Why is that the last minute, there's gray hair. It's liked you become invisible."

- "In retirement, if I want to be active and focused on health rather than illness, I have to be organized, I have to have those things that keep me stimulated, which are goals. I think people are most healthy emotionally, spiritually and physically, when they are valued, contributing and leading purposeful lives."

- "Well, I don't know what I'm going to be up against. I'm curious about what other people's experiences have been. What other people may have gone through during their transition to retirement. What factors did they have when it was a shock to them?  And I know I will miss my peers and the type of work that I'm doing."

- "I would like to hear of more opportunities for people that are retiring. Opportunities for life, such that it can provide a conduit."

- "It is not the change, it is the transition that is the challenge in retirement.  From the time people start thinking about retirement, until they are actually retired, up to the first two years of retirement ... the big transition into their next phase of life."

- "There are very little opportunities in retirement to lessen the fear of change. What people do in retirement - there is not a lot of information out there in layman's terms.  We need somebody who is still actively employed to put together a retirement transition program to address all these different aspects."

These are some of the areas of concern participants expressed.  Future research in these areas would lend itself to assist the baby boomer population as they enter retirement.  An awareness of the trends in an aging population leads to the need for retirement planning.  This aging population will place a huge strain on the Canada Pension Plan (CPP) / Quebec Pension Plan, and with fewer people in the workforce, the Canadian tax base will be smaller. This will further stretch pension programs and the health care system. With this in mind, the focus on financial institutions is increasingly shifting to retirement savings. Because there is less money to go around, it has become more important for Canadians to save and invest wisely. Baby boomers must take charge of their futures or pay the consequences later in life. Unfortunately, most people do not begin planning for retirement until just before they retire. Statistics show that over 60% of Canadians will retire on CPP and old age security alone. The general practice in retirement planning involves estimating the cost of the lifestyle one will likely want to lead upon retirement. Beyond this, individuals must estimate their income needs, taking into account inflation, current assets, and time remaining until retirement. Inflation is a concern because it could potentially erode half of one's spending power in a 15-year period of time.

## For the Organization

People devote enormous amounts of energy to preparing financially for retirement, but too little thought is given to making sure they are psychologically prepared. In a series of studies on mental health and retirement, Kelloway (1994) and co-author Julian Barling, professor in the psychology department of Queen's University in Kingston, found that finances don't predict happiness as much as other factors. This leads Kelloway (1994) to believe that:

> Employers have a bad habit in Canada of offering only financial planning seminars to

prospective retirees...But as retirement approaches, people have to think about what they are going to do with this time... it is the people who get involved and have a sense that they are in control of their affairs who tend to take an active part in planning their retirement. (p. 1)

This research has the potential of making a significant contribution to the body of knowledge on transition to retirement. If the issues are not resolved, we will certainly see and hear of more people suffering through retirement. The research will also benefit many businesses and people. It suggests approaches to leadership that can be of use in the management of change in this era of turmoil and downsizing. It provides information to engage others in a problem-solving process and to display leadership.

## Future Research

- Conduct research to determine what types of workplace environments would be encouraging for people to continue working past the age of 65 years in retirement.

- Conduct research to determine what changes in taxation can be made to encourage retired persons to be more financially independent.

- Conduct research to determine adequate health care facilities and health care options for retired persons.

- Conduct research to determine the needs of retired baby boomers focusing on health, relationships, personal development, life transition or handling change, goal planning and finances.

- Conduct research to redesign retirement communities to meet the needs of retired persons.

- Conduct research to determine opportunities for mentally sharp retired individuals, to encourage the spread of wisdom and value of retired persons in the world.

- Conduct research to consider the application of intergenerational activities in communities bringing together retired individuals as mentors for school children, to encourage career development for children and social respect for the aging population.

- Conduct research to consider combining daycares and long-term care facilities. By doing so, to bring acceptance of older people and display their wisdom to young children. Benefits to older people would then include more fun and zest for life being surrounded by these young children.

- Conduct research to include financial strategies programs in schools to encourage children to start financial planning early.

- Organizations need to better prepare their people for retirement by providing Transitions to Retirement Workshop, focusing on psychological transitions.

# REFERENCES

1.  AI and the Quest - The Quote Center. (1999).
    http://www.appreciative-inquiry.org/AI-Quotes.htm

2.  http://www.appreciative-inquiry.org/AI-Life.htm

3.  Baltes, P. (1987). Theoretical Propositions of Life-
    Span Developmental Psychology: On the Dynamics
    Between Growth and Decline. Developmental
    Psychology (Fall).

4.  Bean, C.R., Layard, P.R.G., and Nickel, S.J. (1983).
    The Rise in Unemployment: A Multicountry Study,
    The Impacts of Population Growth and Aging on the
    Future Canadian Labor Force in Canadian Labor
    Markets in the 1980's. Kingston: Queen's
    University, Industrial Relations Center.

5.  Beehr, T.A. (1986). The process of retirement: A
    review and recommendations for future
    investigation. Personnel Psychology.

6.  Boulmetis, J. (1997). Helping Adults Through their
    Career Transitions. New Paradigms in Adult
    Education. January/February.

7.  Brammer, L. and Shostrom, E. (1977). Therapeutic
    Psychology, 3rd. edition. Englewood Cliffs, N.J.:
    Prentice-Hall.

8.  Bridges, W., (1993). Managing Transitions,
    Addison-Wesley Publishing Company, Reading
    Massachusetts.

9.  Bridges, W., (1993). Making Sense of Life's Changes
    - Transitions - Strategies for coping with the
    difficult, painful, and confusing times in your life,
    Perseus Books, Reading Massachusetts.

10. Bridges W. and Associates. (1992). Managing Organizational Transition. Mill Valley California.

11. Brim, O. G., Jr., and J. Kagan. (1980). Constancy and Change: A View of the Issues" in Constancy and Change in Human Developmen. Cambridge: Harvard University Press. Quoted in [Lerner 1984], p. 23.

12. Bromely, D.B. (1974). The Psychology of Human Aging, 2nd. Edition. Baltimore: Penguin.

13. Central Vancouver Island Health Region (1999). Southern Source. Volume 3, Number 3, March.

14. Central Vancouver Island Health Region (1999). Municipal Pension Plan, Retirement Seminar Handbook.

15. Central Vancouver Island Health Region (1999). Update. September, Volume 3, Number 9.

16. Central Vancouver Island Health Region (1999). Southern Source, Volume 5, Issue 2, February.

17. Central Vancouver Island Health Region website. (1999). http://www.cvihr.bc.ca/

18. Chappell, N. (1998). Maintaining and Enhancing Independence and Well-Being in Old Age. Canada Health Action: Building on a Legacy, Volume 2, Adults and Seniors, Public Health Forum, 1998.

19. Chatelaine Magazine. (1995). Happy Retirement. January, Volume 68, Issue 1, p. 18. Maclean Hunter Publishing Limited.

20. Chiriboga, D. A., and Cutler, L. (1980). Stress and adaptation: Life span perspectives. In L. W. Poon (Ed.), Aging in the 1980's: Psychological issues (pp, 347362). Washington, DC: American Psychological Association.

21. Cimoroni S., Grudzinski B. and Lovett-Reid P. (1997). Retirement Strategies for Women. TD Asset Management Inc. Key Porter Books Limited. Toronto, Ontario.

22. Cullen, Lisa Reilly. (1998). Moves to Make on the Road to Retirement. Money, September 1998, Volume 27, Issue 9.

23. Diamond, P., and Hausman, J. (1984). The retirement and unemployment behavior of older men. In H. Aaron and G. Burtless (Eds.), Retirement and Economic Behavior. Washington, D.C.: Brookings.

24. Dixon, R. (1986). Contextualism and Life-Span Developmental Psychology," in Contextualism and Understanding in Behavioral Science. Ed. M. Georgandi and R. L. Rosnow, New York: Praeger.

25. Dorfman, L.T., Kouhout, F.J., and Heckert, D.A. (1985). Retirement Satisfaction in rural elderly. Research on Aging.

26. Erikson, E. (1963). Childhood and Society, 2nd. Edition. New York: Norton, p. 247-274.

27. Foot, D. (1996). Boom, bust and echo: how to profit from the coming demographic shift. Toronto: Macfarlane Walter and Ross.

28. Foot, D. (1993). <u>Population Aging in the Canadian Labor Force: Changes and Challenge</u>. Journal of Canadian Studies, Volume 28 (1), Spring, 1993.

29. Frankl, V.E. (1963). <u>Man's Search for Meaning</u>. New York: Washington Square Press.

30. Frankl, V.E. (1978). <u>The Unheard Cry for Meaning</u>. New York: Simon and Schuster.

31. Fried, S., Van Booven, D. and MacQuarrie, C. (1994). <u>Older Adulthood - Learning Activities for Understanding Aging</u>. Health Professions Press, Balitmore, London, Toronto, Sydney.

32. Graebner, W. (1980). <u>A History of Retirement</u>. New Haven, Conn.: Yale University Press.

33. Harris, J. (1996). <u>The Learning Paradox: Creating a new security by thriving amid uncertainty.</u> Toronto: Strategic Advantage.

34. Hanisch, K. (1994). <u>Reasons People Retire and their Relations to Attitudinal and Behavioral Correlates in Retirement</u>. Journal of Vocational Behavior, 45, 1-16. Academic Press Incorporated.

35. Herz, D. and Rones, P. (1989). <u>Labor Market Problems of Older Workers</u>. Monthly Labor Review 24, April.

36. Holmes, T. H., and Rahe, R. (1967). <u>The social readjustment rating scale</u>. Journal of Psychosomatic Research.

37. Hutchens, R. (1986). <u>Delayed Payment Contracts and a Firm's Propensity to Hire Older Workers</u>. Journal of Labor Economics, October.

38. Hutchens, R. (1987). <u>A Test of Lazear's Theory of Delayed Payment Contracts</u>. Journal of Labor Economics, October.

39. Keith, J. (1985). Age in Anthropological Research. In Handbook of Aging and Social Science. Ed. Robert Binstock and Ethel Shanas, New York: Van Nostrand Reinhold.

40. Kelloway, K. (1994). Successful Retirement depends on more than Financial Planning. Canadian Press Newswire. July.

41. Kotter, J. (1996). Leading Change, Library of Congress Cataloging-in-Publication Data, U.S.A.

42. Kvale, S. (1996). An Introduction to Qualitative Research Interviewing, Sage Publications, Thousand Oaks.

43. Larson, R. (1978). Thirty years of research on subjective well being of older Americans. Journal of Gerontology, p. 109-125.

44. Lazear, E. (1979). Labor Economics and the Psychology of Organizations. Journal of Economic Perspectives, Spring 1991, Volume 5, Issue 2.

45. Lerner, R. (1984). On the Nature of Plasticity. Cambridge: Cambridge University Press.

46. Marshall, V. and McPherson, B. (1993). Aging: Canadian Perspectives. Journal of Canadian Studies, Volume 28, Spring, 1993.

47. Martin, M. (1999). Leading Organizational Change and Transitions Workbook, Being First Inc. Victoria, B.C.

48. McKay, S. (1998). The age factor: if a company is nothing without its employees who make it work, then surely those with a lifetime of knowledge and

experience must count among its most valuable assets. Journal: Financial Post 500.

49. McNamara, L. (1999). Menopause - Management with Hormone Replacement and Nutritional Supplementation. Orthomolecular Medicine Inc.

50. McPherson, B. (1990). Aging as a Social Process - An Introduction to Individual and Population Aging, Second Edition. Butterworths Canada, Toronto and Vancouver.

51. McTaggart, R. (1991). Principles of Participatory Action Research' Adult Education Quarterly, Vol 41, No 3. Melbourne.

52. Neugarten, B. (1975). The future of the young-old. Gerontologist 15: Part II.

53. Neugarten, B. (1968). Adult Personality: Toward a Psychology of the Life Cycle. In Neugarten, Bernice, ed., Middle Age and Aging. Chicago: University of Chicago Press.

54. O'Brien, G.E. (1981). Leisure attributes and retirement satisfaction. Journal of Applied Psychology.

55. Oshry, B., (1996). Seeing Systems, Berrett-Koehler Publishers, San Francisco.

56. Palys, T.S. (1997). Research decisions. Harcourt Brace Jovanovich. Toronto.

57. Pritchett, P. (1992). The Employee Survival Guide to Mergers and Acquisitions, Pritchett Publishing Company, Dallas Texas.

58. Pritchett, P. and Pound R. (1992). The Employee Handbook for Organizational Change, Prtichett Publishing Company, Dallas Texas.

59. Randall, O. (1977). Aging in America Today - new aspects in aging. Gerontologist.

60. Raphael (1998). Quality of life indicators and health: Current status and emerging concepts.

61. Reason, P. (1997). Political, epistemological, ecological and spiritual dimensions of participation. Paper presented at the World Congress on Action Research and Participatory Research, Cartagena, Columbia.

62. Riddick, C.C., and Daniel, S.N. (1984). The relative contribution of leisure activities and other factors to the mental health of older women. Journal of Leisure Research.

63. Saxon, S. and Etten, M. (1978). Physical Change and Aging. The Tiresias Press, New York.

64. Schein E. (1993). Kurt Lewin's Change Theory in the Field and in the Classroom: Notes Toward a Model of Managed Learning, MIT Sloan School of Management, The Society for Organizational Learning website, U.S.A.

65. Senge, P., Kleiner A., Roberts C., Ross R. and Smith B. (1994). The Fifth Discipline Fieldbook. Doubleday Dell Publishing Group Inc., New York.

66. Sobel, D. Barnes, M. (1991). Go with the flow. New Choices for Retirement Living, Mar91, Vol. 31 Issue 3.

67. Sobel, D. (1991). A New Look at what it really takes to find Happiness in Retirement. New Choices: March.

68. Statistics Canada. (1990). Population Projections for Canada, Provinces and Territories. Ottawa: Statistics Canada.

69. Stringer, E.T. (1996). Action Research: A Handbook for practitioners. Thousand Oaks, CA: Sage Publications, Inc.

70. Thursz, D., Nusberg, C., and Prather J. (1995). Empowering Older People - An International Approach. Published in cooperation with the International Federation on Aging, Auburn House, Westport, Connecticut and London.

71. Tri Council Working Group. (1997). Code of Conduct Involving Humans - Final Report, University of British Columbia.

72. Keith and Paul Van Nosh. (1980). The Best is Yet to Be: Toward an Anthropology of Age. American Review of Anthropology.

73. Victoria Times Colonist Newspaper Article from the Victoria Times Colonist, (1999). Monday May 10, p.A-6.

74. Wadsworth, Y. (1998). What is Participatory Action Research? Action Research International, Paper 2.

75. Waitley, D. (1996). Living in Prime Time - Get the "Max" From Every Moment in Your Life. Phillips Publishing Inc., Potomac, Maryland.

76. We Care Home Health Services. (1998). We Care News - your good health magazine, Issue 2, August. Mississauga, Ontario.

77. Wheatley M. and Kellner-Rogers M., (1999). <u>A Simpler Way</u>, Berrett-Koehler Publishers, San Francisco.

78. Wolfson, M. and Rowe, G. and Gentleman J. and Tomiak, M. (1990). <u>Earnings and Death-Effects Over a Quarter Century</u>. Social and Economics Studies Division, Analytical Studies Branch, Statistics Canada, No. 30.

79. Wolozin, H. (1990). <u>Retirement as an Institution</u>. Journal of Economic Issues, December 1990, Volume 24, Issue 4.

80. Wolozin, H. (1981). <u>Earlier Retirement and the Older Worker</u>. Journal of Economic Issues 15 (June).

81. Wolozin, H. (1989). <u>Culture Psychology, and Institutions</u>. Paper presented at the Annual Meeting of the Association for Institutional Thought, Albuquerque, New Mexico, April 1989.

82. Woodruff-Pak, D.S. (1988). <u>Psychology and Aging</u>. Englewood Cliffs, NJ: Prentice-Hall.

# INDEX

Printed in the United States
74807LV00003B/160

9 781552 124420